The College Student's Research Companion

Second Edition

by
Arlene Rodda Quaratiello

Neal-Schuman Publishers, Inc.

New York   London

Published by Neal-Schuman Publishers, Inc.
100 Varick Street
New York, NY 10013

Printed and bound in the United States of America

Library of Congress Cataloging-in-Publication Data

Quaratiello, Arlene Rodda.
   The college student's research companion / Arlene Rodda Quaratiello.—2nd ed.
     p. cm.
   ISBN 1–55570–385–2 (alk. paper)
   1. Library research—United States. 2. Report writing. I. Title.
Z710.Q37   2000
025.5'24—do21   00–028370
                                               CIP

Contents

PERMISSIONS

Academic Search Elite via EBSCOhost © EBSCO Publishing. Reprinted with permission.

Dialog@CARL homepage © CARL Corporation. Reprinted with permission. Dialog@CARL is a product of the CARL Corporation.

FirstSearch homepage © OCLC. Reprinted with permission. "FirstSearch" and "OCLC" are registered trademarks of OCLC Online Computer Library Center, Inc.

InfoTrac *Expanded Academic ASAP*ô © 2000 The Gale Group. Reprinted with permission.

LEXIS-NEXIS *Academic Universe* © LEXIS-NEXIS Group. Reprinted with permission.

LycosÆ advanced search screen © 2000 Lycos, Inc. LycosÆ is a registered trademark of Carnegie Mellon University. All rights reserved. Reprinted with permission.

"Moon" from "The Nine Planets Multimedia Tour" © William A. Arnett. Reprinted with permission.

Netscape Communicator browser window © 1999 Netscape Communications Corporation. Reprinted with permission.

Northern Light search screens © 1997–2000 Northern Light Technology, Inc. Reprinted with permission.

Reader's Guide to Periodical Literature and WilsonWeb Art Index search page © H.W. Wilson, Co. Reprinted with permission.

SilverPlatter PsycINFO Webspirs © 1967–2000 American Psychological Association, © 1990–2000 SilverPlatter International N.V. Reprinted with permission.

Snap.com Web pages: Copyright © 1997–2000 Snap and its content providers. All rights reserved. The NBC peacock and the NBC Logo are registered trademarks of the National Broadcasting Company, Inc. All rights reserved. Reprinted with permission.

List of Figures and Tables

FIGURES

TABLES

ACKNOWLEDGMENTS

I would like to acknowledge all the Neal-Schuman staff who worked on this book, especially my editor Michael Kelley and the editor of the first edition, Charles Harmon. I also want to thank my husband Mark for his support and encouragement and my daughter Grace for being the world's most patient baby while I wrote this second edition.

Preface

I wrote *The College Student's Research Companion* to serve as an instructional aid for librarians. It was also written out of empathy for freshman and other students unfamiliar with academic libraries. I remember walking into the library as a college student back in the final days of the card catalog era. The sight of all those books made me feel a bit dizzy (or was it, perhaps, that awful dining hall food?). Although I went on to become a librarian, back then my research experience was on par with the average college student (in other words, very little). There was certainly a fair share of time spent wandering aimlessly and wasting time unsure of where to start.

One research assignment in college demanded my first retrieval of a book from the compact shelving. As I walked in to get the books, the shelves literally started closing in on me. The potential headline of the student paper flashed before my eyes: "Crushed in the Stacks!" Would my college career come to a sudden halt at that moment? Fortunately, I pushed the shelves apart long enough to escape. Although this book can't guarantee tips on quick escapes from dangerous shelving, it will help students master the research process. My hope is that all students can learn to avoid any figurative feelings of being "crushed" by their assignments.

The College Student's Research Companion is a "user-friendly" guide explaining the fundamental principles of academic library research. These principles can be applied to all college libraries regardless of the size of their collections or the variety of their electronic resources. The basic research theories covered stand the test of time. Over the past three years, the changes brought about by the unprecedented rise of the World Wide Web have made a new edition necessary so that *The College Student's Research Companion* remains of utmost use to students of the twenty-first century.

The underlying concepts about research emphasized in the first edition are illustrated in this new edition with more pertinent examples and updated information. For instance, most online catalogs are now Web-based so the chapter on searching online catalogs has been revised. Also, many more online databases are now available to students, including LEXIS-NEXIS *Academic Universe* and Dialog@ CARL, so descriptions of these and other new resources have been added. And because students rely more strongly on the Web these days, the section on evaluating information has been expanded to include more detailed criteria for evaluating the content of Websites. These are just some of the changes that have been made to enhance the usefulness of this book.

While *The College Student's Research Companion* has been revised to reflect developments in information technology, it continues to uphold the philosophy that information should be judged for what it conveys, not how it is conveyed—in other words, for its content rather than its format. As students increasingly turn to computerized resources, this philosophy is more relevant than ever. They need to understand that an older article on microfilm may prove more valuable for a certain project than a recent article found through an online service; conversely, a search of the Web may indeed answer a question more effectively than the print materials available in a particular library. Selecting sources regardless of their format results in higher quality research and better research papers.

Even though the Web may appear to have made things easier, in actuality the library (both real and virtual) has become a more complicated place. This book guides students through the maze of resources available and takes them through the research process, step by step, from initial topic selection to citing resources in a bibliography. An introductory chapter discusses topic selection and provides an overview of research. Chapters Two and Three focus primarily on book resources, covering online catalog searching and library classification systems. This is followed by an overview of print and computerized reference sources. Chapter Five discusses how to find periodical articles using indexes in both electronic and print formats. The next two chapters focus on two aspects of electronic resources: how to choose them and how to use them. Chapter Seven, which covers advanced database searching techniques, can also be considered an extension of the earlier discussion of online catalog searching in Chapter Two. The next-to-last chapter is concerned with searching the Web, and the book wraps up with a discussion of evaluating and citing resources.

For schools fortunate to have credit courses in library skills, *The College Student's Research Companion* can serve as a textbook. It can also help to alleviate the frustration of instructional librarians who struggle with "one-shot" lectures. With the increasing complexities of information technology, there is barely time to touch upon essential principles in a single class period; it's even getting difficult to cover everything in a semester-long course. By reading selected parts of this book, students can come to library instruction sessions with a common background so that you can make the most of the time available. They can continue to consult it on their own since there will be so much that you will not have time to discuss.

Throughout *The College Student's Research Companion*, I draw many comparisons between doing library research and going on a road trip. This metaphor was inspired by my fond memories of the "extended study breaks" my college pals and I would often take to escape campus pressures. We'd hop in somebody's car and head off to some destination, whether it be to admire the foliage in autumn or go to the beach on a warm spring day. Although superficially, a road trip and a research paper would seem to have nothing in common, as you'll see in this book there are some surprising similarities.

Research is a journey of discovery that can be just as exciting and stimulating as a trip to an unknown destination. Too many students are intimidated or bored by library research. This book is intended to be a travel guide of sorts— a guide with a somewhat humorous tone that will make the library (both real and virtual) a less intimidating place. With the techniques students will learn by reading this book, they can find their way in the unfamiliar surroundings of college libraries so that doing research will become a positive and enjoyable experience.

One

Hitting the Road

A freshman majoring in computer science is taking a sociology course to fulfill a requirement and has a paper due in about two weeks. The paper must discuss some aspect of human behavior and society. Having chosen a topic, he goes to the librarian at the reference desk in his college library for help:

Student: I'm writing a research paper about the "Y2K bug" and society's reaction to it in the late 1990s . . . you know, like the way everyone was worried that all the computers would crash and people hoarded water and were afraid to fly and that sort of thing. And then I want to examine the actual effects and how it wasn't really so bad after all. Could you show me how to find information on this topic?

Librarian: That sounds very interesting. Let me show you the online indexes for finding articles and then we can see if there are any relevant books yet.

Another student, who is in the same class, reluctantly goes to the library two weeks later (the night before his paper is due) and hesitantly goes to the reference desk after wandering around the library aimlessly for some time:

Student: Um . . . I don't know how to use the library . . . I have a paper due tomorrow and I can't find anything . . . I tried surfing the Web in my dorm room but

1

that was a waste of time. Where are the sociology books? My professor says I need scholarly articles too.

Librarian: Well, the first thing you have to do is choose a topic. I can help you much better then. Do you have any ideas?

Which student do you think will have more success in doing research and a more pleasant library experience? The choice seems pretty obvious.

CHOOSING YOUR DESTINATION

In my experience, the students who seem confused and over-whelmed by the idea of doing research are the ones who don't really know what they're looking for in the first place. Many students walk into the library with a paper assignment and no idea what to do next. The first thing you should do to avoid frustration in the library is to clarify with your professor anything that you don't understand about the assignment. Then you need to come up with a topic that you can be enthusiastic about.

I believe that the most crucial step in the research process is defining what it is you're looking for, just as you first choose a destination when planning a trip. This is necessary to establish a firm foundation. Both students mentioned earlier have been given the same assignment: to write a research paper on some topic relating to human behavior and society. The first student has selected a narrow topic to write about, probably something that holds some personal interest for him. He has a clear idea of where he's headed. The second student hasn't nailed down a topic yet, and so he has no idea what information he really needs. He thinks that if he goes to the library and browses through the section of books concerned with sociology he'll find what he needs. But he's probably going to have a difficult time, especially since he's starting the night before the paper is due.

When selecting a topic, it's always wise to choose something that will engage your curiosity—something that will motivate you when the going gets rough. When you plan a trip, for example, you naturally are drawn toward a place that appeals to you. In the same way, pick a paper topic that appeals to you. Think about the discussions in your class that were interesting, something that you read in a textbook that you would like to pursue further, or just something of personal interest. Brainstorm ideas with your friends and classmates.

Even if you're not given a great deal of latitude in choosing a topic for a particular class assignment, you can come up with a "twist" that will make researching the assigned topic interesting. Relate it to something that does interest you. For instance, the first student in the previous example is really interested in computers. He's taking the sociology class to get a core requirement out of the way. So he relates the given assignment to computers. For another example— let's say you have to do a paper about some aspect of ancient Greek civilization. Unless you're a history or classics major, this assignment probably doesn't sound too thrilling. But perhaps you are interested in sports. How about doing some research on the ancient Olympic Games and the role that sport played in Greek society?

Once you feel that you have zoomed in on an interesting subject, take the following steps:

1) Write down a brief statement of your topic. For example: "Society's overreaction to the Y2K bug in the late 1990s and its actual effects." This step is really quite simple. These topic statements might eventually serve as your paper's title.
2) Below this topic statement, write down the major research questions that you'll want to answer, as well as some preliminary thoughts. To continue with our example, here are a few questions that the student will need to address:

- What is the Y2K bug? How did it arise? Find out the history of the problem and how computer scientists went about solving it.
- Why were people apprehensive about it? Did it have anything to do with apprehension over the new millennium and society's over-reliance on computers?
- How did people react? Find out more about the survivalist mentality, stocking up on provisions, refusal to fly or use elevators, abandoning use of computers, etc.
- What were the actual effects of the Y2K bug? Compare the dire predictions with the actual outcome.

If you can write all of this down in a coherent manner, you'll have a clear understanding of your needs. The process of writing will also make your destination more concrete.

You don't have to pinpoint your topic to the minutest detail. In fact, if you're too narrow in your selection, you will limit yourself. Finding the balance between too broad and too narrow is an art that is often mastered through trial and error. You may find that once you start your research, your original topic will evolve into something different from what you had imagined. Something you come across in your reading may take you down another road. But such detours don't have to take you out of your way—in fact, they often take you on a shortcut to your ultimate goal.

Just remember, if you have no idea where you're going, you'll probably never get there. This holds true on the road as well as in the library.

PLANNING YOUR TRIP

After you've determined your topic, you are ready to map out your route. In other words, you should:

- identify the types of sources that will provide you with the information you need
- determine where and how you will find these sources
- estimate how much time you will need to do your research

Why should you have a plan? Well, without one, you'll probably end up wasting precious time browsing through the library. Although browsing can be effective in the very preliminary phase of research by helping you select a topic and perhaps find some general information, it's not a very good method to use once you've chosen a topic—especially if your topic is very narrow. So think of browsing as a joyride—you have no particular destination but you may see some interesting things along the way. I have nothing against browsing—in fact, I love to browse. But I have observed some students who come in the day before a paper is due and try to get information by surfing the Web, flipping through issues of magazines, or wandering through a section of the library that seems to have books relating to their subjects. This usually doesn't work very well.

Types of Sources
Books

When you think of a library, what's the first thing that comes to mind? Despite the prevalence of computers and electronic resources, books are probably what you picture first, and books do make up the bulk of just about all library collections. There are two main types of books in the library: circulating ones—those you can check out—and reference books—those you must use within the library. These collections are generally kept in two separate areas of the building and are arranged by Library of Congress or Dewey Decimal call numbers.

Although a growing number of students seem to have developed an aversion to books and prefer to rely on electronic sources, nothing is likely to replace the book for depth of coverage as well as accuracy and authority of information— at least not as long as you're in college. Books must go through a rigorous editorial process before being published. Facts must be checked and sources of information confirmed. While anyone can publish on the Web, you usually have to be considered an expert of some sort to have a book published. So if you want to gain a thorough knowledge of your topic, you must at least check to see if there are any relevant books available. You don't have to read these books cover-to-cover; maybe there's just one pertinent chapter. Review the table of contents and index to determine which parts of a book to focus on.

The definition of a book has become open to some interpretation in this electronic age. Some books are also published in electronic format—usually these are reference sources like encyclopedias, dictionaries, and handbooks which are useful for obtaining quick and concise factual information on a broad range of topics, or classic works such as the Bible or *Moby Dick* which are no longer restricted by copyright. But only a very small number of sources originally published in book form are actually available via the Web. I think one reason for this is the discomfort that many people experience when reading computer screens for a long time. Books cover topics in-depth and are, by nature, lengthy publications that require some patience and reflection on the part of the reader. Many books would not transfer well to an electronic format. But I admit that I could be just as wrong as those who believed that the automobile would never replace the horseless carriage. The fact remains for now, however, that if you overlook your library's book collection you're really missing out on a lot.

Periodical Articles

Finding articles in periodicals is another essential component of doing research. Periodicals consist of any publication that comes out on an ongoing basis. As with books, there is generally some sort of editorial process that gives the material validity. As any writer will tell you, it's easy to have an article rejected from a periodical and often takes a good deal of persistence to get published.

Types of periodicals include:

- newspapers
- popular magazines
- scholarly journals

The difference between popular magazines and scholarly journals will be discussed at greater length in Chapter 5. Although it is difficult to draw a line distinguishing the two, and the terms are often used interchangeably, the main difference is that when your professors require you to use journal articles rather than those in magazines, they mean to find publications of a more scholarly nature. The word "magazine" usually indicates a publication of a lighter sort for a more general audience while the word "journal" is more often used when referring to an academic source. But the distinction can be blurry.

Sometimes periodicals provide the only useful information on very narrow or very current topics. For example, before the turn of the millennium there were thousands of articles written about the dreaded Y2K bug, but not very many books since the outcome was still uncertain.

Websites

When I refer to the Web as a source of information, I am not talking about the sources available on the Web that were originally published in other formats—namely, periodical articles that you can obtain through Web-based indexes. I am referring to sources unique to the Web. While evaluating the information you find in book and periodical sources has always been important, evaluating Websites is crucial. As mentioned before, anyone can put anything on the Web.

Sites often lack depth, authority, and accuracy. Although it's hardly the global electronic library it's hyped up to be by the media, there is a great deal of interesting material available on the Web, and it can a be a good source of quick information. However, proceed with caution.

Of course, a library provides more than just books, periodicals, and Web access. There are other types of informational resources: videos, government documents, conference papers, dissertations, maps, photos, and other graphical material. Many libraries have special collections which may relate in some way to the college curriculum or local history. These resources often can't be pigeonholed into the broad categories above. Sometimes there is overlap and you will find references to these kinds of items while searching for books, periodicals, and Websites. For example, some libraries include non-book material in their online catalogs, while government documents are covered in various indexes.

How and Where You Will Find These Sources

Once you have pinpointed your informational needs, you'll require the means to fulfill these needs—just as you'd need a car to get to your destination. To do effective research, you have to know how to use the traditional library as well as the virtual one. In addition to knowing the basics of how libraries are organized, you will find it helpful to utilize online catalogs, electronic indexes, and Web search engines.

In the first part of this book, I'll explain how to use an online catalog most efficiently to find books on your topic. If your library's catalog is not yet available via the Web, chances are it soon will be; so my examples will focus on searching Web-based catalogs. But even older forms of electronic catalogs operate according to similar procedures. From these catalogs, you obtain titles and call numbers. The next step is getting your hands on the books. So I'll take you on a tour through the stacks—those rooms filled with shelves and shelves of books—and explain how everything is organized. Finally, I'll point out the most useful reference books for college students' research papers.

To find articles in periodicals, you don't just browse through issues of magazines or journals or surf the Web hoping to find the complete text of an article on your topic. You first need to select the appropriate index or indexes. Each index covers a different set of periodicals. There are indexes that cover very broad ranges of subjects and others that focus on more narrow disciplines. Often there is a lot of overlap. Most indexes are available in electronic form, making them much easier to use than their print predecessors. But to find articles from periodicals published before the 1990s, you usually have to rely on print indexes. There are many indexes from which to choose. You should become familiar with which ones are available in your library and determine the most appropriate ones to find articles pertaining to your topic.

To find Websites, you must know how Web search engines work. Surfing the Web, like browsing in the library, can be very ineffective. Just as online catalogs enable you to find books, and periodical indexes help you find articles, search engines locate Websites. The only problem is that the development of these tools is in its infancy. When you use a search engine, you often find a lot of irrelevant material. Part of this is due to the amount of junk that is on the Web, part of it is due to ineffective use of the search engines, and part of it is due to the design of the tools themselves. To quote Forrest Gump, search engines are "like a box of chocolates, you never know what you're gonna get." You can't control the content of the Web or the way the search engines work, but you can learn to use them as effectively as possible.

Learning how to use all of these resources isn't something you want to do right before a paper is due. You didn't learn how to drive a car for one particular trip. You learned to drive so that you would have a practical skill for life. In this "information society" we live in, finding information is also a skill you must develop to be successful in life. So you should become familiar with the library even before your first assignment is given. Even if you don't have a particular project yet, stop by the library and get acquainted with it. Try out all of the electronic resources. Practice using your library's computers by looking up a subject of personal interest. What's your favorite TV show? Look it up in the electronic indexes and see what the critics have to say. Where would you like to go for spring break? See if the library has any books about this destination.

Don't be shy about asking librarians for help. Their job is to assist you with any questions you have and your tuition pays their salaries, so take advantage of their services. Go on a tour, if one is being offered, even if you think it might be a bore—you'll be glad you did later, even if all you remember is the location of the most comfortable study space. If you are given the opportunity to go with one of your classes to an instructional session, don't choose that day to cut class—you'll be sorry when the rest of your classmates breeze through their research. Finally, of course, read the rest of this book. The time you invest now in learning how to navigate through the library will save you a great deal of frustration in the future.

Using Other Libraries

Planning your route will also involve decisions such as whether to use the resources of another library. Since not every library can buy every book or provide access to every periodical source, you may have to go elsewhere for the material you need, particularly if another college library has a special collection that relates to your subject. Many smaller academic libraries have limited budgets and select books based upon the academic programs of the school. So a college that specializes in technology will have a lot of science books, but maybe not such a great collection in literature and the fine arts. Your library might be a member of a consortium—a group of libraries in the same area that share re-sources. You can also get materials that you need through interlibrary loan (ILL), a service available at just about ev-ery library that locates a hard-to-find book or article else-where in the country and delivers it to your library. This is a helpful service, but you have to allow a week or two for the material to arrive.

Planning Your Time

Another important aspect of the planning stage is determin-ing how long you will need to do your research and com-plete your paper. Although waiting until the last minute is a common practice, you should expect to be particularly stressed if you do this. The research process is a time-con-suming one, no matter how many time-saving hints I give you.

There are two phases to completing a research paper: do-ing the research and writing the paper. Too often, students dismiss the research process as that boring task they have to get over with in the beginning. Research is a major com-ponent of a research paper; that's why it's called a *research* paper. Without material, you have nothing to write about. Good research results in papers that will get high marks from your professors. I believe it should take one-third to one-half of your time to do the research, depending on how adept a writer you are.

Although computers are a tremendous aid, they don't just spit out the exact information you need without some men-tal effort on your part. And you can't get all the informa-tion you need on a computer screen. Although an increasing number of computer databases provide the text of articles on-screen and electronic versions of entire books are avail-able on the Web, you'll most likely have to get your hands on a lot of the material you need. This requires time and ef-fort.

The length of the paper as well as your own research experience will, of course, determine when you should start your research. I have no mathematical formula to offer concerning how many days you'll need to complete a certain number of pages. My primary recommendation is that you allow yourself time for roadblocks along the way: a book you need has been checked out; you realize that you'll have to go to another library or get a book through interlibrary loan; the computer system has crashed—there are any number of scenarios. Sometimes your gut instincts tell you when it's time to start. A mild anxiety may come over you. Since the cure for worry is action, just getting started will make you feel better.

Set aside a short time for an initial visit to the library well in advance of your paper's due date. Promise yourself you'll spend an hour on your research but don't put any pressure on yourself. You don't even have to be successful in finding anything. Just go. Chances are you will have positive results. Then go again the next day. Spend some time each day working on your research. Take small steps and you'll see that slowly everything will come together. This really works—in fact, it's the approach I took in completing this book.

ABOUT THE EXAMPLES USED IN THIS BOOK

The car in which you learned to drive may not be the car you drive now. But because all cars operate according to the same principles, you'll find that things are fundamentally the same: you put your foot on the gas pedal to make the car accelerate or on the brake to slow down or stop; you turn the wheel to steer. Sure, little things are different: on a dark night when it starts to rain and you're borrowing a friend's car, you may curse as you search frantically for the windshield wiper controls or defroster. And you'll probably need a few extra lessons to learn how to drive a standard transmission if you're accustomed to automatic. In the future perhaps, as you sit behind the wheel of your flashy new electronic automobile, you might look upon the car you drove in driver's ed as an antique, but the lessons you learned in that gas-powered vehicle should still be easily transferable.

The examples used in this book can be like that driver's ed car. Although you may not use exactly the same resources in your library, the examples I have chosen demonstrate fundamental principles that will enable you to use the particular resources that are at your disposal.

It is unavoidable that in the rapidly changing world of information technology the sources I cover will undergo minor as well as drastic modifications by the time you read this book. But I believe that most of these changes will be superficial, just as the look and performance of cars has been altered over the years but the way you drive them hasn't changed very much. That's why it's so important to understand the basic theories of doing research rather than the specifics.

Perhaps you have had the disconcerting experience of visiting a Website one day and returning the next to find that the site looks completely different. Computers are constantly being upgraded and—supposedly—improved, but this leaves the average user feeling confused and a bit intimidated. My purpose, therefore, in using certain examples will be to demonstrate the fundamentals that endure rather than giving specific instructions that might change by next week. With the knowledge of the underlying theories, you will have a road map that will lead you through unfamiliar territory.

CONSIDER THE ROAD LESS TRAVELED

A final point I would like to make before proceeding to the specifics of how to use the library concerns how you choose resources; this point also relates to my discussion of books earlier in this chapter. Computers have certainly revolutionized the library. Electronic periodical indexes, multimedia reference sources, and the World Wide Web have changed the way research is done in countless ways. Some of these changes are good, but others, in my opinion, are not. The main problem that has arisen with the emergence of computerized resources is that many students have come to rely exclusively on computers. These students ask questions like "Why read a book?" and "Why track down old journal articles on microfilm?" I counter by asking, "Why limit yourself?" There is still plenty of information that is not available electronically and may never be. You should choose your resources based on content rather than format; in other words, judge a resource for its informational value rather than whether or not it's available on the computer.

This issue reminds me of a road trip I took with a friend of mine in Arizona. One beautiful spring afternoon, we drove off to "get our kicks on Route 66," the first highway constructed between Chicago and California back in the 1920s. It remained the major east-west route until the superhighway Interstate 40 was built parallel to it in the 1970s. Now Route 66 has become a byway, a back road that is traveled by tourists who have time to sightsee rather than drivers who are in a hurry to get somewhere. But with all its roadside pit stops, hamburger joints, neon signs, teepees, ghost towns, and other quirky attractions, Route 66 is a much more interesting road to travel than I-40, which looks like just about every other superhighway in America.

Similarly, computerized resources have paved a superhighway through our libraries. Traditional resources remain but are often overlooked. As you read this book and utilize the techniques discussed in it, keep in mind that the best resources might not be the easiest to get. It may take you a little more time to find that obscure journal article or book, but it may well be worth it. Remember what Robert Frost wrote: "Two roads diverged in a wood, and I—I took the one less traveled by, and that has made all the difference."

Two

The Key to the Online Catalog:
Database Searching Basics

You probably don't even remember the card catalog; it has become a relic in most libraries, about as outdated as a station wagon in this era of SUVs. The online catalog has become the tool for finding books and other materials that a library holds. Basically, the online catalog is a computerized version of the old card catalog with some added features. Since the majority of online catalogs are now available via the Web, the examples in this chapter will utilize a very generic Web catalog that should reflect whatever system you will use in your library, even if it is an older one.

Because you will probably need to search the catalogs of other libraries at some time, which can easily be done on the Web, it is useful to understand the basics that underlie all systems. The catalog of another library may be just a mouse-click away. There is also the possibility that your library—especially if you're at a small school—shares its catalog with other libraries in the area.

We start with learning how to use the online catalog because most research should begin with finding books. As I mentioned in the previous chapter, books are an excellent source of authoritative and in-depth information. Remember, however, that online catalogs include other material besides books, such as CDs and videos. Searching the online catalog is similar to searching any computerized database, whether it is a periodical index for finding articles or a Web search engine for finding Websites. So what I explain here will certainly carry over into other chapters of this book.

THE STRUCTURE OF ONLINE CATALOGS

Each book in a particular library has a *record* in the online catalog (there may also be records for periodicals, videos, etc.). Figure 2.1 is an example of a record for a book. All of these records together comprise the *database* of the library's holdings.

Just as a database is composed of individual records, each record is composed of individual elements called fields. A *field* is a certain type of information about the item. For a

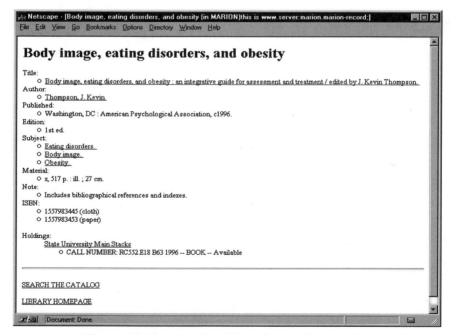

Figure 2.1: An example of an online catalog record.

book, such as the one in Figure 2.1, there are fields for the title, author and publisher. Other essential fields include the subject field, which I will be discussing at great length in this chapter, and the call number, which is so important that I spend the entire next chapter explaining it.

SEARCHING TECHNIQUES

Although the layout and format of online catalogs of different libraries may vary, fundamentally they all operate in the same way. As in the old card catalog days, there are three basic ways of finding books: by title, by author, and by subject. Since the computerization of catalogs, however, a fourth, very useful, way of searching has emerged: keyword searching. Figure 2.2 displays a sample opening screen for an online catalog. By clicking on any of the options you will access the appropriate search screen that will provide a form for entering your search criteria. As you can see, it is also possible to search by numbers such as call number or ISBN, but they are used infrequently.

If you are dealing with a catalog that is not Web-based, things may look and operate differently, but the underlying idea is the same. The main difference is that you must select what type of search you want to perform by entering a command (perhaps "s=" for a subject search) rather than clicking on a link.

Searching by Title or Author

It is easy to find a book if you know the author's name or the exact title. Figure 2.3 displays a typical search form for title searching. You simply enter your title in the box and click "Begin Search." You can also limit the search very easily to the type of material (books or non-books), the language (most useful for eliminating foreign language works), and date. This is a very common feature of Web-based catalogs.

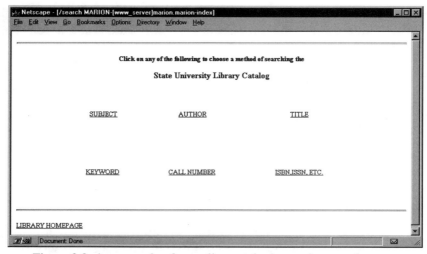

Figure 2.2: An example of an online catalog's opening search screen.

There are a couple of simple conventions to use when searching for books by author or title:

- when looking up an author, use the last name first
  example: **King Stephen** (usually no comma is necessary)
- when looking up a title, the general rule is to drop any articles
  example: *A Tale of Two Cities* should be entered **Tale of Two Cities**

If you do not find what you're looking for, first make sure that you have followed these two rules, then check to make sure that you have the correct spelling and that the author or title you have entered is a valid one. The computer cannot read your mind; contrary to popular belief, it is just a stupid machine that takes all the commands you give it quite literally. By the way, your search can be all in lowercase.

Searching by Subject

Before searching for a book by subject, it is helpful to have a clear idea of your topic. As discussed in the preceding

Figure 2.3: A sample search form for searching an online catalog by title.

chapter, you'll wander aimlessly if you don't know where you're going. While your topic may evolve as you proceed, you do need to have some sense of direction.

Let's say you are doing a paper on eating disorders. Your first inclination would probably be to enter the subject heading **Eating disorders**. If you do this, you will certainly find books if your library has any on the topic because this is a valid heading. After clicking on the search button, you will see subject headings similar to those listed on the screen displayed in Figure 2.4.

In this example, 35 books have been located on the general topic of eating disorders. However, the three lines below this heading—**Anorexia nervosa**, **Bulimia**, and **Compulsive eating**—offer what are known as *cross-references*. Cross-references are often narrower topics that fall under the main subject area, but they can also stand alone. By clicking the appropriate heading, you can perform a separate search for these subjects.

Below the cross-references are *subheadings*. These are also narrower topics under the main heading, but they sub-

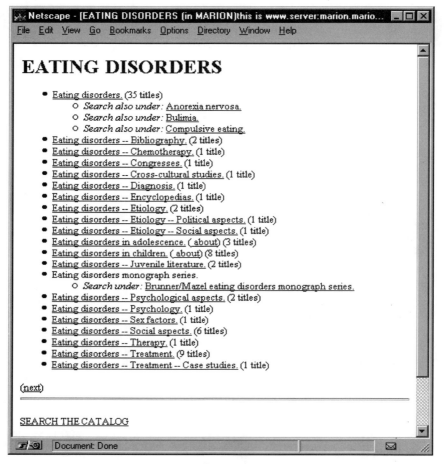

Figure 2.4: An example of a subject heading list in an online catalog.

divide the main heading and cannot stand alone. **Eating disorders—Bibliography** and **Eating disorders—Encyclopedias** denote specific types of books; **Eating disorders—Etiology** denotes a subdivision of the main topic, in this case the study of the causes of eating disorders. This is further divided with sub-subheadings into political and social aspects.

Once you have found the appropriate subject heading, you

are not done. Your goal is to get your hands on some books on the topic. You must delve to the next level to find the individual book records by clicking on the heading you want. This brings up a list of the individual books and other items as shown in Figure 2.5.

This screen gives you some basic information on each item: the author, title, publisher, and year. The location of the item is also indicated as well as its availability. The book may be available, checked out, or have some other status such as non-circulating (a reference book, for example) or on hold.

If you want to see complete records such as the one displayed in Figure 2.1, you need to select a particular title. I recommend that you take a look at some of the full records for one very important reason. If you look closely at Figure

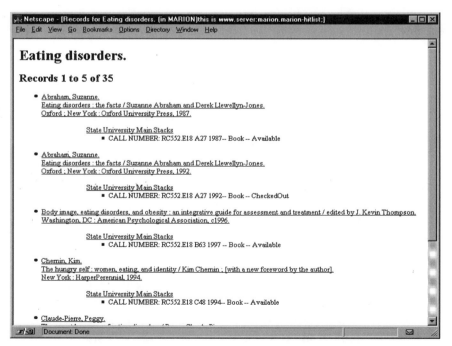

Figure 2.5: A typical online catalog title display.

2.1, you'll notice that the book retrieved has two other subject headings in addition to **Eating disorders**. These are **Body image** and **Obesity**. These subjects may be related to your research topic, so you may be interested in following them further. You can easily do this using a Web-based catalog. Simply click on the subject heading. By clicking the link for **Body image**, you will instantly retrieve the records for all the books on this subject. This is a powerful feature that gives you the ability to explore related material in a very convenient manner.

Subject searching doesn't always work as effortlessly as the previous example might suggest. Sure, **Eating disorders** is a subject heading, but not everything you might think to enter is going to be a heading. It's the same as when you look up a listing in the yellow pages and find that doctors aren't listed under **Doctors** but under **Physicians**. Subject headings are determined by the Library of Congress, which puts together the official list of standard, acceptable headings under which all library material is categorized. The list is actually quite long, occupying the space of four large, red volumes known as *The Library of Congress Subject Headings*, or, simply, the "red books." You've probably seen these large books near the computers in the reference area without giving them a second glance.

If you don't mind leafing through the pages of the "red books," they can help you determine appropriate headings to enter in the online catalog. In the "red books'" alphabetically arranged list, official headings are indicated by bold type. **Television advertising** is one such heading, as displayed in Figure 2.6.

What does all of this mean?

UF—use for—terms that **Television advertising** should be used for. This part isn't too useful, basically telling you, for example, that **Television advertising** should be used instead of **Television commercials**. Conversely, however, if you had looked up **Television commercials**, you would have been told to **USE Television advertising**—this *is* helpful.

Television advertising *(May Subd Geog)*
  ᵣHF6146.T42ᵤ
  UF Advertising, Television
      Commercials, Television
      Television commercials
      Television in advertising
  BT Advertising
      Broadcast advertising
      Radio advertising
      Television broadcasting
  RT Television commercial films
  NT Cable television advertising
      Singing commercials
  — **Awards** *(May Subd Geog)*
  — — **United States**
        UF Television advertising—United
            States—Awards
            ᵣFormer headingᵤ
        NT Clio Awards
  — **Law and legislation** *(May Subd Geog)*
      BT Advertising laws
  — **United States**
  — — Awards
        USE Television advertising—
             Awards—United States
Television advertising and children
  (May Subd Geog)
  BT Children
Television advertising directors
  (May Subd Geog)
  ᵣHF6146.T42ᵤ
  BT Television—Production and direction
Television advertising films
  USE Television commercial films
Television anchors
  USE Television news anchors
Television and baseball *(May Subd Geog)*
  UF Baseball and television
  BT Baseball
Television and children *(May Subd Geog)*
  UF Children and television
  BT Children
Television and copyright
  USE Copyright—Broadcasting rights

Figure 2.6: A sample listing in *The Library of Congress Subject Headings*.

BT—broader term—terms that will retrieve more material or material that covers a broader subject area. For example, **Broadcast advertising** will find material that covers advertising on both television and radio, so you'll probably find more books if you use it or books that have a wider scope of information.

RT—related term—suggestions for other terms you could try; in this example, **Television commercial films**.

NT—narrower term—terms that will limit your search. If you look up **Cable television advertising** or **Singing commercials**, which are narrower subjects, you will find fewer books.

Below all of this begins the list of subheadings you can use with **Television advertising**, which includes **Awards**, **Law and legislation**, and **United States**.

The online catalog will often perform the same function as the "red books," referring you to official headings as well as associated headings. Let's say you were looking for books about the Vietnam War. You'd probably just enter the subject heading **Vietnam War**. Having done this, however, you would see the following reference in our hypothetical catalog: **Vietnam War, 1961–1975** *search for* **Vietnamese Conflict, 1961–1975**. In a Web catalog, cross-references are hypertext links, so you could just click on **Vietnamese Conflict** and easily perform the right search. Although it seems a bit odd that the official heading is **Vietnamese Conflict**, it's not surprising when you remember that the Library of Congress is a branch of the United States Government. Since the Vietnam War was never officially recognized as a war, this is not an acceptable subject heading. But when was the last time you heard someone refer to the "Vietnamese Conflict"? If you search the online catalog for titles that contain that phrase you probably won't find any, but the majority of books on the topic will contain the phrase "Vietnam War" in their titles.

You may also notice an occasional lack of political correctness in subject headings. For example, **Indians of North America** is the official heading for Native Americans. The wheels of the Library of Congress, as with any large bureaucratic institution, move slowly. Headings do change to reflect the times. **Moving picture plays**, for instance, was eventually changed to **Motion pictures**. But you are less likely to find terms in current usage established as subject headings. **Generation X** was only recently added to the list; before that, the term **Baby busters** defined that concept.

Sometimes subject searching can be downright infuriating. If you entered **Motion picture violence**, which is not a subject heading, you would be informed that there are no books on this subject. Often just changing the word order or playing around with the phrase a bit will do the trick. For example, you will find that **Violence in motion pictures** is a valid heading.

Another suggestion is to think of synonyms for your heading. Perhaps, considering the formality of Library of Congress subject headings, you might think to enter **Daytime dramas** to find books on soap operas, when, in fact, the official heading *is* **Soap operas**, despite the colloquial sound of it.

Finding a subject heading that you can use is often a process of trial and error. But it's worth the effort. Despite the apparent ease of keyword searching, as I will explain in the next section, there is no better way to retrieve a complete list of relevant material than by subject searching. We can only hope that someday there will be a similar tool for searching the Web. We'll discuss this in more detail later in the book, but part of the reason you retrieve so much junk when using Web search engines to find Websites is precisely because there are no subject headings assigned on the Web. Because of subject searching, online catalogs can be much more efficiently searched than the Web.

Searching By Keyword

Picture an old card catalog. Hmm . . . Have you ever even seen one? Well, they had a lot of little drawers in which index cards were filed alphabetically under every author, title, and subject of every book in the library. They took up a lot of space and were sometimes a bit unwieldy to use. Now imagine that cards could be added for every single word contained in the titles, authors' names, and the subject headings—not just the first word. In addition, imagine that the space on the cards is without limit so summaries and notes could be added to the descriptions of many of the items and additional cards could be added and alphabetized under each word in these summaries and notes. The card catalog would probably be bigger than the library building itself! Although even more unwieldy to use, this imaginary card catalog would enable you to find more books than you would have the conventional way.

Here's an example. Suppose you are looking for books about headhunters (the kind that can get you a job, not the kind you often see on re-runs of *Gilligan's Island*). If you pull out the appropriate "H" drawer in this massive, imaginary card catalog, you would find cards for books about both varieties of headhunters. But *My Friends, the New Guinea Headhunters* certainly won't serve your purpose. Before this, however, is a card for *How to Answer a Headhunter's Call: A Complete Guide to Executive Search*—again the word "headhunter" is in the title. Since the subject heading under which this book is officially categorized in **Executives—recruiting**, doing a traditional subject search would never have located it, but this keyword search does. You can do this sort of search with an online catalog or just about any other searchable electronic database.

A keyword is any word that appears in a computerized item record, except for common prepositions and articles such as *the*, *of*, *to*, and the like—which are called stopwords—as well as three special terms *and*, *or*, and *not* which serve a special function to be discussed shortly. A keyword could be in the title field, the subject field, the notes field— any field. You can search for single words or phrases, as well as combinations of words and phrases.

Boolean Logic and Using the Connector AND

The real power of keyword searching is demonstrated when you need to look up more than one word or phrase. For example, let's say you can't remember the exact title of the book you need about investing but you know that a famous stock investor whose first name is Peter wrote it. You're pretty sure that "Wall Street" is in the title. You enter the keyword search **peter and wall street**, and through the magic of keyword searching you are able to locate *One Up on Wall Street* by Peter Lynch. You have basically instructed the computer to find all the records that contain both terms.

Keyword searching using more than one term or phrase, such as in the previous example, operates according to the principles of Boolean logic, which were developed by George Boole, a nineteenth-century mathematician. These principles are really very straightforward. Boolean logic can be used to define a topic very specifically, so that from among millions of items in a library you can find the ones that meet your needs. The principles I'll discuss here are extremely important because they form the basis of searching any computerized database as well as using Web search engines effectively.

Keyword searching is invaluable for finding material on multi-disciplinary subjects that are difficult if not impossible to define by one single subject heading. Suppose you wanted books about drug abuse among women. To understand Boolean logic, picture two sets of books: the first contains all the books about women and the second contains all the books about drug abuse. A third set is formed by the books that belong in both sets because they're about both women and drug abuse. When the linking term AND is used, records that contain the two words specified are retrieved. Figure 2.7 illustrates what is happening.

The portion of this diagram in black is the set representing records that include the terms **women** *and* **drug abuse**. The more terms you link together, the narrower your search becomes and the fewer records you will retrieve. For instance, a search for **women and drug abuse and treatment** will retrieve a narrower set, as in Figure 2.8.

The portion of this diagram in black is the set representing records that include the terms **women** *and* **drug abuse** *and* **treatment**. Notice that it is smaller than the highlighted portion in Figure 2.7.

If you don't find any books, or if you only find a few, you can try dropping a term. This will broaden your search. Or, if you get too much, narrow your search by adding a term. You will find that keyword searching can often be a process of trial and error like subject searching.

Using the Connector OR

You can also use the word OR between terms to broaden a keyword search. Picture a set containing all the books about

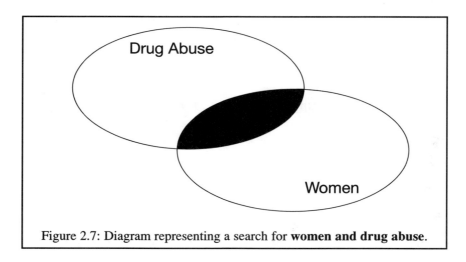

Figure 2.7: Diagram representing a search for **women and drug abuse**.

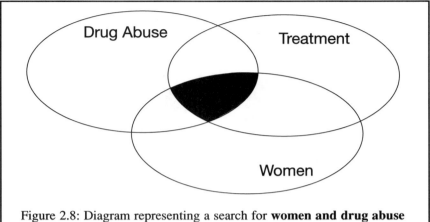

Figure 2.8: Diagram representing a search for **women and drug abuse and treatment**.

air pollution and another set containing all the books about water pollution. Some of these books must certainly overlap in subject material covering both topics. But the set resulting from a search for **air pollution or water pollution** will contain not only the books that address both topics but also those that are about one or the other.

In Figure 2.9, the area in black represents those books that address both topics, but the areas in gray are also included in the resultant set because the connecting term OR was used. If you were to add another term to this search using OR, the outcome would be even larger because the more terms you link together with OR, the broader your search becomes; this is the opposite of what happens when using AND.

Truncation

Truncation can serve a purpose similar to that of OR. With this technique, you drop the ending of a word and replace it with a truncation symbol. This symbol differs among online catalogs and other computerized databases. The ques-

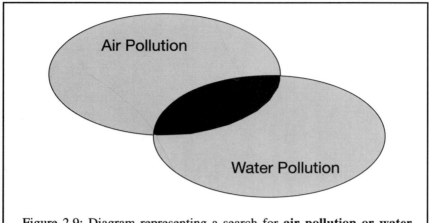

Figure 2.9: Diagram representing a search for **air pollution or water pollution**.

tion mark (?), asterisk (*), and pound signs (#) are frequently used. For example, you could enter **environment?**, which would retrieve all of the records containing any words beginning with *environment*; in addition to *environment* itself, you would also retrieve *environments, environmental, environmentalists*, and so on. Occasionally no symbol is necessary and truncation is automatic.

Truncation is helpful when you want to retrieve both the plural and singular forms of a word; just substitute the catalog's truncation symbol for the "s." You can also use truncation symbols within words to act like a wild card. For instance, if you wanted to find either **woman** or **women**, you could enter **wom?n** which would serve the same purpose as the lengthier **woman or women**.

Once again, truncation is not limited to online catalogs. It is an important concept to understand when searching any computerized database.

Using the Connector NOT

You can use the word NOT between terms to eliminate ir-

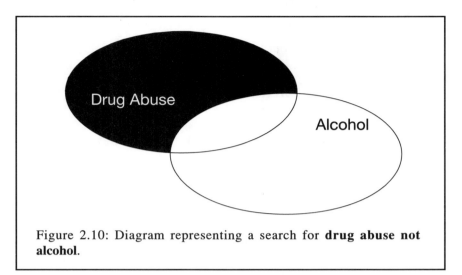

Figure 2.10: Diagram representing a search for **drug abuse not alcohol**.

relevant items. For example, if you wanted to find all the books about drug abuse but weren't interested in those dealing with alcohol, you could enter the search as **drug abuse not alcohol**. This would eliminate all the records in which the word "alcohol" appears, as Figure 2.10 illustrates.

In this figure, the area in black again represents the resultant set, but it is not a part of both original sets, only the set of books about drug abuse. Although NOT is used less often than the other two connecting terms, it can be very helpful in avoiding one of the pitfalls of keyword searching—retrieving irrelevant records.

Combining Connecting Terms

You can combine ANDs, ORs, and NOTs in one search to get really specific. Although my examples here will involve using parentheses, many Web-based catalogs simplify the process with advanced search entry forms. What's important to understand is the theory behind this technique of combining search terms.

For example:

(drug abuse not alcohol) and women

retrieves records concerning drug abuse among women but not alcohol abuse

**children and violence and
(motion pictures or television)**

retrieves records about the effects of violence in both movies and TV upon children.

Using parentheses when combining sets in this way, or entering them separately in the boxes on a search form, defines your search criteria so the computer can sort them out correctly. If I searched for **drug abuse not (alcohol and women)** instead of **(drug abuse not alcohol) and women**, I wouldn't find any books on alcohol or women because the *not* eliminates both words inside the parentheses. **(Children and violence and motion pictures) or television** will retrieve books about children and movie violence as well as *every* book in the library about TV whether or not it has anything to do with children and violence. Just use your common sense when it comes to this more advanced form of keyword searching.

Problems with Keyword Searching

Although keyword searching offers solutions to some of the problems inherent in subject searching, it does have problems of its own.

1) Lack of Comprehensiveness—Keyword searching does not necessarily retrieve every record on a subject. The only way to get a comprehensive list of material is by identifying the proper subject heading. For example, if you look up **y2k bug** as a keyword phrase, you'll only find the records that contain this phrase. These records will all list **Year 2000 date conversion** as a subject heading. Not every book with this subject heading, however, will contain the keywords **y2k**

bug since that's really a slang form of the subject. If you return to traditional subject searching and look up **Year 2000 date conversion** (which is often as easy as just clicking on the subject heading within the book record you have found), you will get a complete list of all the books on this topic.

2) Retrieval of Irrelevant Material—Keyword searching often retrieves irrelevant material because it takes words out of context. If you wanted a book about the architecture of Boston and were to enter **boston and architecture**, in addition to retrieving all the records for books about Boston architecture, you would also retrieve all the books about architecture that were published in Boston but not necessarily about Boston. Remember that basic keyword searching picks up words from all the fields in a record including the publisher field.

3) Retrieval of Peripheral Material—Because keyword searching searches the entire item record that might also include chapter title, notes, summaries, etc. you might also get a lot of books that will contain only a small amount of information on your topic.

Field-Specific Searching

To lessen the effects of the second two problems just mentioned, you could limit your keyword searches to particular fields in a record. Web-based catalogs have certainly simplified this advanced level of searching. For example, for books about Boston architecture, you could indicate that you only want these words located within the subject headings of records and/or within the titles. Limiting keyword searches to subjects and titles is an excellent way to refine your search if you find that you have retrieved too many records or irrelevant records. *Field-specific searching*, as this technique is called, is also very useful when searching electronic periodical indexes as well as when using Web search engines and many other computerized databases that we will be discussing further along in this book.

Now that you know the ins and outs of using an online catalog, take it for a spin and find some books on your topic. The best way to remember the techniques I explain in this book is to actually use them in real-life situations. You would never have learned how to drive a car unless you got behind the wheel at some point, started the engine, and hit the road, no matter how much you had read the driver's manual.

Three

Traveling Through the Stacks

The first time I went into New York City by myself I felt a bit anxious. I was afraid I wouldn't find my friends, whom I had planned to meet near Macy's department store. But my anxiety was a bit unjustified because, despite the immensity of Manhattan, it's not that hard to find your way around. Whoever originally designed the road system laid out most of the streets in a grid-like pattern. So instead of all the streets being uniquely named, most were simply numbered. This makes it possible through a little trial and error to determine if you're going in the right direction, even if you've never been there before.

I had to get to Fifth Avenue and 34th Street—the famous end-point of Macy's Thanksgiving Day Parade—from the Port Authority bus terminal at Eighth Avenue and 42nd Street. This is not the nicest area, by the way, so I was hesitant to ask for directions. I just started walking down Eighth Avenue and the next block happened to be 43rd Street, so I knew I was going in the wrong direction. I turned around. When I reached 34th Street, I took a left because that just felt like the direction to go. When I came to Seventh Avenue, I breathed a sigh of relief. Going two blocks further, I reached my destination.

Libraries can be compared, in a way, to Manhattan. Although usually much quieter, libraries can be big and often overwhelming. When people go into them, they often think it will be hard to find their way around. Libraries these days certainly contain much more than just books, but books still take up the most space, and books are often what you look for when you begin your research. The average college library contains hundreds of thousands of books; a large university library contains millions! But you can easily find what you need amid this overwhelming amount of material if you understand how everything is organized. With this understanding, you will also be able to locate periodicals, videos, and other non-book material in the many libraries that organize these collections in the same way as their book collections. Even some Web directories, such as *CyberDewey* and *CyberStacks*, arrange their listings using the same systems that have been in use for over a century to arrange books in libraries.

THE LAY OF THE LAND

There really weren't too many libraries before the nineteenth century, except for those catering to the needs of academic institutions and individuals who could afford to pay dues. Each one of these private libraries organized its books in a different way. But in the 1800s, several factors—all related to the Industrial Revolution—led to the rise of libraries. A more technologically literate society was needed to support the rise of industry, so public education and literacy became widespread. At the same time, technological advances in printing, which transformed it from a manual to a mechanical process, made the production of books less expensive and easier. Finally, Andrew Carnegie and other leaders of industry donated large sums of money to support the building of new libraries. With more books, more people reading them, and more libraries, there was a greater need for a standard system of organization. Two systems actually emerged: the Dewey Decimal Classification, used in many public libraries and some smaller college libraries; and the

Library of Congress (LC) Classification, the standard in larger public institutions and most academic libraries.

In order to get your hands on the books you have identified in the online catalog, you need to be familiar with either the Library of Congress system or, less frequently, the Dewey Decimal system, depending on which is used by your library. Students constantly come to me for help because they can't find a book (which is fine, librarians are there to help); but in many cases they need help simply because they don't really understand the system that is used to arrange them. There are probably countless other students who don't ask for directions, but instead just wander through the stacks wasting precious time and getting frustrated. To avoid getting lost in the stacks, here's a crash course in what is called *classification*.

Every book in a library is given a unique number—a *call number*—to indicate its location. You find out a book's call number by looking it up in the library's online catalog. With Dewey Decimals, as well as the LC Classification, the subject matter and the author's name determine the number a book is given, which in turn determines its location on the shelf.

THE DEWEY DECIMAL CLASSIFICATION

The Dewey Decimal Classification divides knowledge into ten broad categories from 000 through the 900s (see Table 3.1). Each broad category is subdivided into ten more sections, which are each further subdivided into ten smaller sections and so on until you get down to the level of individual books that will have call numbers involving decimals. For example, if you are interested in literature, the books you want are located between 800 and 899. More specifically, books of American literature are between 810 and 819. This is further subdivided into sections such as poetry, drama, and essays, each designated by a whole number. Nineteenth-

Table 3.1 Dewey Decimal Classification

000–099   **General works**—like encyclopedias, but a lot of other topics have been thrown in over the years ranging from Bigfoot and UFOs to computers and the Internet.

100–199   **Philosophy**—this also includes psychology, astrology, witchcraft, and related topics.

200–299   **Religion**—200–289 includes Christianity, while all other world religions are crammed into the 290–299 section.

300–399   **Social science**—includes sociology, political science, economics, and related topics.

400–499   **Languages**—here you will find books about individual languages as well as linguistics in general.

500–599   **Natural sciences** (as opposed to applied sciences, which are covered in the next section)—books on mathematics, astronomy, chemistry, physics, and life sciences are found here.

600–699   **Technology**—includes applied sciences ranging from medicine and engineering to cooking.

700–799   **Fine arts**—includes painting, sculpture, music, performing arts, television, games, and the like.

800–899   **Literature**—includes classic literary works as well as literary criticism, but does not usually include contemporary fiction and other works not considered "classic" (these are generally kept in a separate fiction section arranged by author).

900–999   **History**—in addition to historical topics, includes biographies which are all kept in the 920 section.

century American writers are found within the 818 section. A copy of Henry David Thoreau's classic *Walden* has the specific call number 818.31. To summarize the hierarchical scheme:

800–899 Literature
  810–819 American literature
    818 Nineteenth-century American literature
    818.31 Thoreau's *Walden*

The part of the number following the decimal point can be a bit confusing. Just to review some basic math (you didn't think library research was going to involve math, huh?), decimals don't have the same value as whole numbers. For instance, *Walden*, as well as books about *Walden*, at 818.31 will actually be found after a book with a number like 818.2987, because .31 is more than .2987. When using decimals, zeros get dropped, so .31 is really the same as .310 or .3100 and so on to infinity. When zeroes are appended, it's easier to see that .3100 is greater than .2987.

The Dewey Decimal Classification has some inherent weaknesses. Its hierarchical scheme has a strong bias toward Western culture as well as a lack of concern for what we refer to today as "political correctness." A similar situation is obvious with the emphasis on American, British, and Western European literature. The literature of countries that were considered alien to most people in nineteenth-century America—Asian, African, and Middle Eastern countries as well as Russia, Poland, and many others—is squeezed between 890 and 899.

Another problem with this system is that, as new subjects arise, they must be shoehorned in somewhere; the original nineteenth-century scheme had no place for topics such as computer programming and television. Computer books have been thrown in with the encyclopedias, and you'll find the books about television along with all the books on movies in the fine arts section, specifically 791.4 (not even a whole number!). Because of this, books in these and other unforeseen areas must have long and complicated call numbers in order to give each a unique location.

THE LIBRARY OF CONGRESS CLASSIFICATION

The Library of Congress Classification is more complex. It is used by some larger public libraries, many academic libraries, and, of course, by the Library of Congress, which designed it in the nineteenth century to organize the increasing number of books in its collection. This national library has grown from a small, one-room, legal collection established in the Capitol in 1802 for the use of Congress to a massive institution that contains over one-hundred million items. Such a vast collection requires a more specific scheme of organization; Dewey Decimals are not sufficient for the task.

The LC Classification breaks all of knowledge down into twenty broad categories indicated by letters of the alphabet (see Table 3.2). You'll find encyclopedias in the A section, atlases in the G section, and literature in the P section. You may think it's odd that Military and Naval Science are considered top-level categories, but you have to remember that the original purpose of the scheme was to serve the needs of the government. The basic categories are subdivided alphabetically. For example, while books on literature are given the letter P, English literature is PR and American is PS.

The LC system is alphanumeric. Following the initial one, two, or, occasionally, three-letter code are numbers that further divide a particular topic. If you're looking for humor (which you may be needing if you've gotten this far in the chapter), go to the PN6160s. A particular book like Jerry Seinfeld's *Sein Language* has the call number PN6162 .S358. How would you go about getting your hands on this item? Locating the book on the shelf is akin to locating Fifth

Table 3.2 Library of Congress Classification

A **General works** such as encyclopedias.

B **Philosophy**, **religion**, and **psychology**.

C **History**—special topics like archaeology, genealogy, and general biography.

D **World history**.

E/F **American** and **Canadian history**.

G **Geography** (mostly)—in addition to atlases and books about various geographic areas, you'll also find books about the environment, dancing, and sports.

H **Social sciences**—includes sociology, economics, and business.

J **Political sciences**.

K **Law**.

L **Education**.

M **Music**.

N **Fine arts**—includes painting, sculpture, and architecture.

P **Literature**—also includes theater, movies, and television.

Q **Natural sciences**—mathematics, astronomy, chemistry, physics, life sciences, and so on.

R **Medicine**.

S **Agriculture**.

T **Technology**—other applied sciences like engineering, photography, and cooking.

U **Military science**.

V **Naval science**.

Z **Bibliography**—library science as well as bibliographies that list materials on various subjects.

Avenue and 34th Street in Manhattan since the books are all shelved in a certain order. But the Library of Congress system is more complicated than this analogy implies because, like the Dewey Decimal Classification, it also utilizes decimal points as well as an often confusing jumble of letters and numbers. It's more like getting to Macy's, finding the shoe department, and selecting a pair of shoes in your size.

So you want to get a copy of *Sein Language* at PN6162 .S358. Here are the steps to take:

- First, you have to find out where the P section is located. Consult a floor chart or ask your friendly librarian who will be much more approachable than many of the characters you'll find in the Port Authority bus terminal.
- Once you find the general P section, finding the PNs is simply a matter of alphabetical order—they'll be between the PMs and the POs.
- When you find the PNs, follow the call numbers numerically until you get to 6162. Don't confuse this with the Dewey system and look for 616.2. If you try looking for PN616.2, you'll wind up in a totally different section from PN6162 and see lots of books about classical, medieval, and renaissance literature—certainly not what you had in mind.
- In your continuing quest for PN6162 .S358, you switch back to the alphabet to find S (which stands for the author's last name).
- After finding the S section, you encounter the trickiest part of the LC Classification: the dreaded decimals. You need to look for .358 (just drop the S now that you've found it). Recalling our discussion of decimals earlier in the chapter, would *Sein Language* at PN6162 .S358 be found before or after a book called *You Have a Hang-up If . . .* which has the call number PN6162 .S37? Is .358 greater than .37? No, because .37 is the same as .370, which is obviously greater than .358.

What about a book called *Copycat* at PN6162 .S2513? If you've got a grip on decimals now, you'll have no problem determining that *Copycat* will be found before *Sein Language*. To make sure this is all clear, let me list the order in which you'd find the books:

    PN6162 .S2513   *Copycat*
    PN6162 .S358   *Sein Language*
    PN6162 .S37   *You Have a Hang-up If . . .*

At first glance, you might have thought that these books would actually go in the opposite order, but if you just insert some mental zeros, it becomes clear that this is the proper arrangement.

The year of publication is often included at the end of the call number, but I have omitted it here so the numbers appear a bit less daunting. This date is only important in distinguishing one edition of a book from another.

I admit I've gotten into some picky details here. In reality, what often happens is this: you find the general section you need, such as PN6162, and then, realizing that the books in this section are arranged by author's last name, you simply scan the titles on the shelf to find what you need rather than straining your eyes looking at those little call numbers on the book spines. This can work effectively in many situations.

Library of Congress call numbers, however, are not always as simple as in the humor section. I mentioned before that when classification systems were developed in the nineteenth century, many subjects did not even exist. So when books about airplanes, television, and in-line skating were written, they had to be fit in somewhere. As a result, a lot of books have been crammed into very small call number ranges and therefore must have very long call numbers with lots of digits, letters, and decimals.

For example, let's take a look at the section of the library that contains books about the Internet. Although a decade ago you would probably have found no books about the

Internet in most libraries, now there are thousands, and all of them are designated by the call numbers starting with TK5105.875 .I57. A particular book like *The Complete Idiot's Pocket Reference to the Internet* has the lengthy call number TK5105.875 .I57 G65. If you break down this call number, it's really not too much harder to find than *Sein Language*; it just looks more intimidating.

- After finding TK and 5105, you look for .875 the way you look for any decimal.
- Then you find .I57 by first locating the Is and then .57.
- Finally, after finding G (which stands for Goldman, the author's last name), you regard 65 as a decimal also even though there's no decimal point before the G. In the LC scheme, any number after the initial whole number is regarded as a decimal. So *The Internet for Windows* by David C. Gardner at TK5105.875 .I57 G368 will be found before TK5105.875 .I57 G65.

There is another confusing aspect of the LC Classification. Where's the fiction section? Libraries that use LC numbers don't have a separate fiction section as do public libraries using Dewey Decimals. This is because the LC scheme is intended more for research than for recreational purposes. All fiction is put in the literature section (designated by call numbers beginning with P), side by side with criticism of the various works. The same is true for biographical material; whereas Dewey libraries put all biographies in the 920s, LC libraries have them scattered throughout the collection depending on the occupation of the person about whom the book is written.

Many books are hard to classify because they might involve more than one subject. A book about the psychology of women, for example, may be classified in the HQ section rather than BF, which is the primary psychology section, because HQ contains books on women's studies. Depending on how the cataloger looks at the book, it could fit in either section. If this book on the psychology of women was of a more medical nature, it could even be placed in the RCs. If there's only one copy of the book, however, it can only have one distinct call number, the cataloger must make a choice. This same problem can occur when a book is classified with the Dewey Decimal system. This is why it is important to use the online catalog rather than just meandering through the stacks; you may find that books on basically the same subject are in different call number areas.

Once you get familiar with the system used to organize books, however, you can do some "educated browsing." Although, in Chapter 1, I said that browsing is not an effective way to do research, if you practice "educated browsing" in certain call number areas, you often serendipitously find some useful material. Of course, if you're looking for something really narrow, you may have problems. Restrict your browsing to more general information on a topic. To be an "educated browser," look up your subject in the online catalog and find a few relevant books and their call numbers. Then, after locating these books in the stacks, take a look at what other books are on the shelf nearby.

As a side note, another way to find further material once you're in the stacks and have found a few books is to look in the back of each of these books for a bibliography of sources. If you notice any titles in the bibliography that look pertinent, look them up in the online catalog to see if your library has them.

I mentioned that both the Library of Congress and Dewey Decimal Classifications were developed as indirect responses to the Industrial Revolution. As we undergo another period of change, the Information Revolution, these two systems still serve to give some order to what could easily be chaos. In fact, there are a growing number of Web directories that organize material based on these schemes. For example, as I mentioned earlier in this chapter, *CyberDewey* is a site that categorizes many other sites using the Dewey scheme. The designer of this site, David A. Mundie, who is not a librarian, explains why these traditional classification systems still deserve our attention, "It became clear that library classifications were ideally suited to my organizational needs. They have evolved over a long period of time to solve exactly the sorts of problems that confronted me, and they embody a tremendous amount of collective wisdom."[1]

Notes

1. David A. Mundie. 1995. "Organizing Computer Resources," *CyberDewey. users.telerama.com/~mundie/CyberDewey/CyberDewey.html,* 1/10/00.

Four

Stopping for Directions: Reference Sources

Imagine getting lost while driving through a desert. It's the hottest time of the day, and the road ahead of you stretches on for miles; you're not even sure if you're going in the right direction or if you should have gone left at that last fork in the road. You're running low on fuel, you can't find a map in the glove compartment, and, to top it off, you're getting thirsty! It's been fifty miles since you passed a gas station and you have no idea how long it will be before you come to another.

This situation is what comes to mind when I think of students who must complete those library "scavenger hunts" which require them to answer a series of trivial questions using reference sources. The intention is good—to learn how to use the library's resources, especially the reference room—but the result is usually a frustrated student who can't wait to leave the library. You shouldn't be sent to the library to complete such an assignment or any research project without some clear directions. That's what this chapter will give you.

Reference sources enable you to find quick answers to your questions as well as broad information on paper topics to either get you started with your research or check a fact before handing in your final draft. They are the basic necessities of research, just as water and fuel are indispensable when driving through the desert. In this chapter, I'll introduce you to the major categories of reference sources by posing some trivial yet fascinating questions and then showing you how to find the answers effectively. If you encounter a similar sort of question in the future, you'll know where to go. This chapter will not inundate you with lists of book titles accompanied by dull descriptions. Instead, I will highlight the types of sources that I consider among the most helpful and give you a few examples.

The reference room, however, can no longer be considered just a physical place in the library building because many reference books are now available online or on CD-ROM and more are becoming available all the time. Libraries increasingly provide access to computerized reference sources through their Websites, which provide links to Web versions of sources. For example, the venerable *Encyclopaedia Britannica* has a very popular Website at *www.britannica.com*. Despite the difference in format between print and computer versions, however, the content remains very similar in the emerging virtual reference room.

We'll be discussing the evaluation of Websites later on, but a few words are appropriate here. If something is available for free, it's usually of a lower quality and/or includes a lot of advertising. Libraries must subscribe to most of the good computerized resources I will discuss just as you subscribe to cable TV to get commercial-free programming. So be a bit cautious when using the Web for reference sources. And be extremely skeptical if you feel the urge to simply use a Web search engine to find the answer to your question—you will probably retrieve a lot of irrelevant junk and even inaccurate information (but more about that later). If your library's Website provides links to Web-based reference sources, these sources have probably been selected because of their quality. Your library often has to pay a fee for these sources and restricts access to the college's own students.

No college library will have every source mentioned here, but a good library will have a large percentage of them, as

well as many other titles that fall into the general categories of reference material described in this chapter.

ENCYCLOPEDIAS: A GOOD STARTING POINT

Q: How much did the *Titanic* weigh? What was the name
     of the ship that came to her rescue?

A: The *Titanic* weighed 46,328 tons. The ship that rescued
     the survivors was the *Carpathia*.

Source: *Encyclopedia Americana*, 1994 International ed., s.v.
"Titanic."

Encyclopedias, whether computerized or in their traditional place on the bookshelves, are often a good place to
start your research because they provide concise, factual
overviews on a vast number of subjects. Encyclopedias are
probably one of the first things that come to mind when you
hear the term "reference books." You will usually find the
volumes of general encyclopedias in the A call number section of the reference room if your library uses the LC Classification or in the 030s if Dewey is used, along with other
general works.

The most scholarly and in-depth encyclopedia is
Encyclopaedia Britannica. Here are others you are likely to
find:

- *Encyclopedia Americana*—suitable for college-level research.
- *Academic American Encyclopedia*—also a good starting point for your research projects.
- *Collier's Encyclopedia*—written on a high-school level,
  this encyclopedia is intended for a more general audience.
- *World Book Encyclopedia*—this should be a last resort
  because it is not intended for college-level research.

Many encyclopedias are now available online. In addition to *Encyclopaedia Britannica*, there is Microsoft's *Encarta Online* encyclopedia (*www.encarta.msn.com*), which has no print equivalent. Using *Encarta*, you can find answers to the *Titanic* questions but you also have to look at a bunch of ads. And in order to access all the information available, you have to be a paying subscriber.

The Importance of Consulting the Index

Often, the most important part of an encyclopedia or any reference source or book is its index. Without it you may never find what you need. The following question demonstrates this situation:

Q: Who were the Plastic People of the Universe?

A: No, they weren't Saturday morning TV cartoon characters. This was the name of a Czechoslovakian band whose members were arrested in the mid-1970s along with other intellectuals, artists, and students who belonged to the Charter 77 movement for Czech independence, which protested the repressive measures imposed after the Soviet invasion. The band's arrest motivated the playwright Vaclav Havel and others to sign a manifesto demanding respect for human and civil rights.

Source: *Encyclopedia Americana*, 1994 International ed., s.v. "Czechoslovakia."

The answer is in the C volume of *Encyclopedia Americana*, not the P volume. If your subject is not in the appropriate lettered volume, it's probably not broad enough to have its own entry in a general encyclopedia. Look it up in the index, which is the last volume of the set. If you look up Plastic People of the Universe in the index, you are directed to volume eight (the C volume) under the heading "Czechoslovakia."

The index is also handy because you can locate all the entries relating to your topic, not just the one that starts with a particular first letter. For instance, if you look up "deserts" in the index volume of *Encyclopedia Americana*, you'll be referred to a number of subtopics in different volumes that all relate to the main topic, such as specific places (Death Valley and the Mojave Desert) and related topics (cactus, oasis, and the infamous dust devil—a mini-tornado filled with sand). This will give you more information than would be contained in the D volume alone. It's similar to the online catalog providing you with cross-references for books.

Indexes are the key to using the book versions of most reference sources, and are also helpful in finding information in many nonfiction books in the circulating collection. If you're having trouble finding the information that you need in a particular source, chances are there is an alphabetical index either in the back of a one-volume source, or in the final volume of a multivolume set (like a general encyclopedia) that will indicate on which page to locate your information.

Before you start saying, "What a pain, let's go to the computer," you might be interested to know that many electronic reference sources utilize a computerized version of a back-of-book index. They are not indexes in the traditional sense. You might think that since databases are searchable by keywords that an index would be unnecessary, but users are starting to realize that they can wander just as aimlessly through a Website as through a book, so site designers are incorporating indexes into their products. They serve the same purpose. Instead of turning to a certain page in a book, however, you click on a link and go to a particular page within a site.

Subject-Specific Encyclopedias: Off the Main Drag

Q: How did the mood ring, that short-lived jewelry fad of the 1970s really work? And why did Sophia Loren's mood ring make tabloid headlines in 1975?

A: Inside the stone of the mood ring were heat-sensitive liquid crystals derived through a chemical process from sheep's wool, the same stuff that had been used for years in hospital thermometers. In 1975, Sophia Loren stopped a press conference because to her horror her mood ring had turned black—a very bad omen, indeed!

Source: Jane and Michael Stern, *The Encyclopedia of Bad Taste* (New York: HarperCollins, 1990), 218.

I couldn't find any entries for mood rings in traditional general encyclopedias, and I checked four different ones. This is where subject-specific encyclopedias sometimes come in handy. The subjects covered by the *Encyclopedia of Bad Taste* include a variety of fads of the 1970s such as mood rings, disco, and bell bottoms (which experienced a recent revival), as well as the short-lived phenomena of other decades.

Whereas each major general encyclopedia consists of many volumes, specialized encyclopedias are often just one volume, although some are multi-volume sets. Besides finding topics that may not be covered in general encyclopedias, these specialized books can go into much greater depth. More common specialized encyclopedias include the *Encyclopedia of Philosophy*, the *Encyclopedia of Religion*, and the *Encyclopedia of Popular Music*. Think of any major subject area and there's probably an encyclopedia that focuses on it.

There are also encyclopedias that focus on narrower subjects. In addition to the *Encyclopedia of Bad Taste* cited above, you might also find such offbeat titles as the *Star Trek Encyclopedia* and the *Encyclopedia of Unbelief*. How do you locate these helpful sources? I'll reiterate a technique that we've discussed before that will come in handy here—keyword searching. For example, if you want to find out if there is an encyclopedia about sleep in your library, enter the keyword search **encyclopedias and sleep** in the online catalog. This works well when looking for any subject-specific reference source. If you need a timeline of women's issues, try a search for **chronologies and women**; if you need a film term defined, search for **dictionaries and motion pictures**.

Sometimes encyclopedias have confusing titles that use the word "dictionary" instead of encyclopedia. For example, the *Dictionary of American History* is a multivolume work that I wouldn't describe as a dictionary because of its length and depth of coverage. Ordinarily, the basic difference between an encyclopedia and a dictionary is in the length of the entries: a dictionary implies brief definitions, while an encyclopedia contains lengthier essays. The line between these two types of sources sometimes gets a little blurry.

DICTIONARIES: WHAT DO YOU MEAN?

Q: What are the following: 1) phrenophobia, 2) soogie-moogie, 3) the best boy?

A: 1) Phrenophobia is a "morbid fear of having to think, endemic to politicians, or a morbid fear of losing one's mind" (common also to many college students).

2) Soogie-moogie is a slang term for a "mixture containing soda used for cleaning paintwork and woodwork on boats" (not to be confused with sudzy-dudzy or squeegie-weegie).

3) If you've ever sat through the closing credits of a movie, you've probably wondered what the best boy does. Basically, he or she is the chief assistant to the chief electrician (or gaffer) on a motion picture set.

Sources:
1) Stuart Sutherland, *The International Dictionary of Psychology* (New York: Continuum, 1989), 325.
2) John Ayto and John Simpson, *The Oxford Dictionary of Modern Slang* (Oxford: Oxford University Press, 1992), 232.

3) Ira Konigsberg, *The Complete Film Dictionary* (New York: New American Library, 1987), 27.

Aside from the usual language dictionaries you may consult from time to time, like *American Heritage* or *Webster's*, there are numerous specialized dictionaries such as those used above. As mentioned before, it's sometimes hard to draw the line between encyclopedias and dictionaries, but you could also consider these mini-encyclopedias providing brief definitions of terms used in a particular field of study in an alphabetical format. There are many dictionaries available via the Web (many are listed at *www.rcls.org/deskref/ Dictionaries*).

ATLASES: BEYOND WHERE

Q: What were the five largest American cities in 1790? In 1870?

A: Philadelphia was actually the largest city in 1790, followed by New York and then Boston, Charleston, and Baltimore. New York had overtaken Philadelphia by 1870; Brooklyn (which is today considered part of New York City) was third, followed by the more westerly cities of St. Louis and Chicago.

Source: Kenneth T. Jackson, ed., *Atlas of American History* (New York: Scribner's, 1984), 97, 177.

Atlases are commonly used to find out where a place is, how to get to it, what its geographic features are, etc. This is handy for many research purposes and most students are familiar with the straightforward atlases that are basically books containing maps of physical places. But atlases come in other varieties also. The question above reveals the usefulness of atlases that provide historical information. There are also atlases that focus on certain themes, such as the *At-*

las of the Supernatural. Although the maps are usually supplemented with more text than a general atlas, at the heart of these books are the maps that relate geography to a particular subject.

STATISTICAL SOURCES: HOW MUCH? HOW MANY?

Q: Which is the more popular pet in the United States: the cat or the dog?

A: Among the entire population of the United States, the dog wins this contest when counting the actual number of households with pets; in 1996, 31.2 million households had a dog while 27 million households had a cat. However, the average number of dogs owned by each household was 1.7, while the average number of cats was 2.2. So, the actual population of pet cats in the United States was 59 million while that of dogs was 52.9 million.

Source: *Statistical Abstract of the United States* (Washington, D.C.: U.S. Government Printing Office, 1998), 262.

Statistical Abstract of the United States is a good place to check for any sort of national statistical information. It is an annual collection of statistics derived from the government census as well as from private sources. When you locate the appropriate table, be sure to note the year of the information given. Just because you're using the most recent volume doesn't mean you're getting the most recent information; the pet statistics, you will note, are from 1996. *Statistical Abstract* is also available online at *www.census.gov/prod/www/statistical-abstract-us.html.*

Q: What percentage of U.S. households have at least one television set? How about in Angola?

A: Of all U.S. households, 98 percent own at least one

television (34 percent have two; 40 percent have three or more); in Angola, there are 48 TVs for every thousand people—a rate of 4.8 percent.

Source: *World Almanac and Book of Facts* (Mahwah, NJ: Funk and Wagnalls, 1998), 188, 762.

If you require statistics for another country, a good place to check is the *World Almanac and Book of Facts*. Although this source includes primarily U.S. information, there is a long section that contains a brief entry for each country.

Other helpful sources for more in-depth international information:

- *Statesman's Yearbook*
- *Country Studies* (also available at *http://lcweb2.loc.gov/ frd/cs*)
- *CIA World Factbook* (also available at *www.odci.gov/ cia/publications/factbook*).

The U.S. government is an excellent provider of statistical information and most of it is now available online. In addition to *Statistical Abstracts* and the sources listed above you can find a wide range of reliable sources at *www. fedstats.gov*. Government sources are also good because they are free. I don't include too many Website addresses in this book because most of the reliable reference sources are fee-based and your library may not subscribe. But government sources are available to anyone with Web access.

CHRONOLOGICAL SOURCES: WHEN?

Q: When was the first successful circumnavigation of the earth in a balloon? How long did it take and who accomplished this milestone?

A: On March 20, 1999, Dr. Bertrand Piccard of Switzerland and Brian Jones of Britain went around the world in nineteen days, one hour, and forty-nine minutes, becoming the first balloonists to successfully circle the earth.

Source: "Round-the-World Balloon Flight Succeeds," *Facts On File World News Digest*, 25 March 1999: 199.

Facts On File World News Digest is a news service that provides biweekly summaries of world events. It's an excellent source for not only finding out when something happened but also who did it and other key information. In the print version, the digests are collected in a binder throughout the year and then bound up into annual volumes. Your library might also subscribe to *Facts On File* on the Web via the *FACTS.com* Website.

Q: In what years did the following motion picture "firsts" occur: 1) sound movie, 2) Academy Awards, 3) drive-in theater, and 4) psycho-slasher film?

A: 1) 1927 (*The Jazz Singer* with Al Jolson)
2) 1929 (not a very suspenseful event since all the winners were announced in advance)
3) 1933 (in New Jersey)
4) 1978 (*Halloween*)

Source: Bruce Wetterau, *New York Public Library Book of Chronologies* (New York: Prentice Hall, 1990), 552–557.

For events of a more historic or thematic nature spanning a number of years, such as motion picture history, chronological reference sources are very helpful. There are numerous books covering different historical topics, or themes such as American wars (*Chronology of World War II*) or women's history (*Chronology of Women's History*). Try the keyword search method in the online catalog to find these sources (for example: **chronology and world war ii** or **timeline and world war ii**). There is also an excellent book called *Time-*

tables of History that, for any given year, will indicate what was going on simultaneously in politics, art, society, and more.

BIOGRAPHICAL SOURCES: WHO ARE YOU?

Q: When was Mark McGwire, the homerun hitting record holder, born? For what team did he play the year he hit 70 home runs, smashing Roger Maris's record?

A: McGwire was born on October 1, 1963. He was a member of the St. Louis Cardinals in 1998, the year he became "homerun king."

Source: *Who's Who in America*, 53rd ed., s.v. "McGwire, Mark."

This is just one of the many *Who's Who* books, which also include *Who Was Who in America* (for famous deceased people), *Who's Who in Show Business*, *Who's Who Among Women*, and so on. What all of these books have in common is an alphabetical format that contains very brief entries on notable people. There is usually contact information of some sort (not in the *Who Was Who* books, obviously), and all the important dates and accomplishments in the person's life.

Q: How did Picabo Street, the Olympic skier, get her unusual first name?

A: Her parents, true flower children of the 1960s, had intended for their daughter to choose her own name when she was old enough. When they applied for passports, however, they were informed that "Baby Girl" was not acceptable as a name, so they chose a place name meaning "shining waters" in the language of the Sho-Ban Indians of Idaho. Their daughter loved playing peekaboo and, although not a Native American, was a third generation Idahoan so it seemed like an appropriate name to them.

Source: *Current Biography Yearbook* (New York: H. W. Wilson, 1998), 556–559.

If you want more in-depth information on a notable person, one place to turn is *Current Biography*. This series provides biographical essays on people who made an impact on the world in a particular year in some field—perhaps politics, sports, or entertainment. It is available both online and in print.

There are many other sources for biographical information in the typical reference collection, some of which may focus on a particular country, ethnic group, time period, or occupation. There are two that I consider worthy of special mention because I find myself directing students to them time after time. The *Dictionary of American Biography* covers figures of note in American history—always popular paper topics. And since biographical information on writers is always in such high demand, *Contemporary Authors*, which provides biographical sketches on current writers, and its companion series, *Dictionary of Literary Biography*, which contains lengthier essays on writers living and dead, are highly used. *Contemporary Authors* is now also available online.

DIRECTORIES: GETTING IN TOUCH

Q: Who is the director of the Society of Earthbound Extraterrestrials, and how can I contact him/her?

A: The director's name is Otamer Tllak. But unlike E.T., don't "phone home"; contact him at the headquarters of the society at 780–444–UFOs.

Source: *Encyclopedia of Associations*, 35th ed. (Detroit: Gale Research, 1999), 1:751.

Real people are great sources of information. Let's say you're doing a research paper on UFOs and you want to interview someone to add pizzazz to your paper. Or maybe you just want to be sent some literature in the mail on a particular organization or find out the address of its Website. To identify organizations, learn their missions, and find out how to get in touch with them, use the *Encyclopedia of Associations* (also available online or CD-ROM). This is not an encyclopedia in the true sense; it is more accurately defined as a directory, since it directs you to something.

Other useful directories:

- *Who's Who in America:* we've already looked at this series as a source of biographical information but it is also a directory since it provides contact information
- *United States Government Manual:* how to contact appropriate governmental agencies and officials

QUOTATION SOURCES: SAY WHAT?

Q: Who said the following?
1) "The most beautiful thing we can experience is the mysterious. It is the source of all true art and science."
2) "I learned three important things in college—to use a library, to memorize quickly and visually, and to drop asleep at any time given a horizontal surface and fifteen minutes. What I could not learn was to think creatively on schedule."

A: 1) You may know this man by his more famous quote, "E=mc2"—Albert Einstein
2) Agnes de Mille, the famous choreographer, in her book *Dance to the Piper*.

Source:
1) *Bartlett's Familiar Quotations*, 14th ed. (Boston: Little, Brown, 1968), 950.

2) *The New York Public Library Book of 20th Century American Quotations* (New York: Warner Books, 1992), 165.

Books of quotations serve three purposes:

- to find quotes pertaining to a particular theme
- to find some quotes attributed to a particular person
- and, conversely, to find out who said a particular quote

There are two basic varieties of quotation books: thematically arranged and chronologically arranged. The best-known book of quotations is *Bartlett's Familiar Quotations*, which belongs to the latter type although you can also find quotes on specific themes by looking up keywords in the index.

The source for the quotation from Agnes de Mille is a thematically arranged quotation book. Such compilations are great for finding a quote to use on a specific subject but not so useful in identifying the source of a quote.

BIBLIOGRAPHIES: WHERE DO I GO FROM HERE?

Q: What books were written about the Beatles between their rise to stardom in the early 1960s and their disbandment at the end of that decade?

A: Over thirty books were written, including such memorable works as *The Beatles: A Study in Drugs, Sex, and Revolution*, which contended that these four lads from Liverpool were really part of a communist plot to take over the world, and *Up the Beatles Family Tree*, a genealogical study of the Fab Four.

Source: Roman Iwaschkin, *Popular Music: A Reference Guide* (New York: Garland, 1986), 226–232.

Although you might think of a bibliography simply as the list of sources at the end of a book or as the list you must compile for your own research paper, there are also a wide variety of book-length bibliographies to be found in the typical reference room. These books can be enormously helpful because they are focused on one particular subject and provide citations for books, periodical articles, audio-visual material, and rare unpublished works relating to the subject.

As you can see, the reference room, whether real or virtual, is an oasis where your thirst for information can certainly be quenched. I have only scratched the surface in this chapter. The reference librarians at your library can assist you in using the sources I have mentioned and can suggest other resources that might be helpful in your research.

Five

Finding Your Way Through Periodicals

You certainly shouldn't head out on a long road trip without a map, especially if you're concerned about arriving at your destination on time or without getting lost. The purpose of maps is to show you the way—to guide you on your journey. Similarly, you shouldn't begin your search for periodical articles without first consulting a periodical index. These indexes, as I'll detail in this chapter, are like road maps for finding your way through periodicals, helping you to determine which issues will contain articles on your topic. Wandering around the periodical room and browsing through issues of magazines and journals is a highly ineffective way to search for articles. You will certainly feel lost if you proceed in this manner. And if you believe that Web search engines will lead you to the sources you need, think again; articles from published sources are rarely available on the Web for free. The most efficient way to find articles is to use periodical indexes.

As I emphasized in Chapter 1, the first step on the road of research is defining your topic. So before you go about searching indexes for articles, it's a good idea to have your subject chosen. It's okay to have a broad topic, but, as you proceed with your research, you will have to hone in on a specific idea to pursue.

TYPES OF PERIODICALS

The next thing you have to decide is what type of articles you need. Although one thing all periodicals have in common is that they are published on an ongoing basis (daily, weekly, monthly, or quarterly), there are different varieties of periodicals: scholarly journals, trade journals, general magazines, newspapers, etc. Before proceeding further, I should explain some of the important differences between types of periodicals since they, along with your topic, will determine which indexes you search.

The terms "journal" and "magazine" are often used synonymously. When your professors instruct you to find journal articles, however, they usually don't have *People*, *Time*, or *Cosmopolitan* in mind. Professors generally want their students to use scholarly journals in their research; these are periodicals containing articles written by experts in particular fields of study, frequently individuals affiliated with academic institutions. Scholarly journals tend to be very specialized in their subject focus and are research oriented, containing examples of primary literature sources. Primary sources are those in which scholars who have conducted research report their findings (as opposed to secondary sources which report on someone else's activities). Another characteristic of academic journal articles is that they are often "peer reviewed." This means that before an article is accepted for publication, it must be deemed worthy by a group of the author's colleagues. Academic journal articles usually have bibliographies at the end citing all the sources referred to in the text; this can be very helpful, leading you to a variety of sources that may aid in your research. There is another type of journal that is useful to those doing business research—the trade journal. Trade journals are periodicals written for people working in a specific industry.

The term "magazine," on the other hand, brings to mind general-interest publications that you would find on any newsstand. Magazines are intended for a general audience and don't go into as much technical depth as scholarly journals. They may be easier and more enjoyable to read, but they are usually not as valuable for your own research. If you picked up a copy of *People*, you might see articles such as "The 50 Most Beautiful People in America" and "Richard Gere: Sexiest Man Alive." Were you to look at the table of contents of an issue of the *Journal of Popular Culture*, however, you'd see articles like "Law as Soap Opera and Game Show: The Case of *The People's Court*," "Yes, Virginia, There is a Gender Difference: Analyzing Children's Requests to Santa Claus," and "Frankenstein as Founding Myth in Gary Larson's *The Far Side*." The difference in content is obvious. The physical difference is also apparent. Magazines tend to be glossy publications with eye-catching covers while journals are often more dull looking—but don't judge a periodical by its cover.

INDEXES: YOUR ROAD MAPS FOR FINDING ARTICLES

In Chapter 4, I pointed out that the index in the back of a book is a very important tool. Instead of browsing through the entire book looking for what you need, you simply turn to the alphabetically arranged index in the back of the book and look up your subject to determine what page to turn to. Periodical indexes do the same sort of thing by referring you to articles in specific issues of various periodicals. There are many different indexes, each one focusing on periodicals in a particular subject area.

Most often today, you will go to a computer to use an index. These electronic indexes will provide not only references to articles, but often the text of the articles themselves. In the past, students had to rely on print indexes to find articles. Unlike the card catalog which can be considered obsolete, print indexes still serve a purpose, as I'll explain later.

A Basic Example of an Electronic Index

The following is a very simple example of how you would find articles using an electronic index. It utilizes InfoTrac's *Expanded Academic ASAP*, a very popular periodical index in libraries today. Most online indexes have a similar structure. The next chapter describes some of the other common electronic databases, you are likely to find in a college library and will highlight a wide variety of other indexes you might use. Chapter 7 will go into greater detail on how to search computerized databases, including indexes. For now, I just want to give you a general idea of how you go about finding articles.

Suppose you needed to find articles about Mount Everest. If your library subscribes to InfoTrac, it is probably just a click away on the library homepage. InfoTrac is a service that provides a collection of indexes each focusing on a different subject. By selecting *Expanded Academic ASAP*, which covers hundreds of academic journals as well as popular magazines, the opening search screen will be displayed as shown in Figure 5.1.

In the search box you enter the subject **Mount Everest** and click "search." As a result, the screen displayed in Figure 5.2 appears.

It starts by listing the heading you're looking for; this is followed by all the other headings starting with **Mount Everest**. Underneath each heading you can click on the word "View" in order to see the citations for the articles pertaining to that heading. The main heading for Mount Everest also has the option to "Narrow by subdivision." This basically provides you with subheadings that you can search individually; I will explain this further in a moment. For now, clicking "View" brings up a screen containing a list of citations, as displayed in Figure 5.3.

The citations are listed in groups of twenty in descending chronological order—that is, most recent first. A citation

Figure 5.1: Opening search screen for InfoTrac's *Expanded Academic ASAP*.

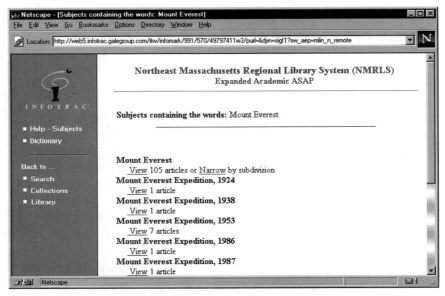

Figure 5.2: Subject listing for **Mount Everest** in InfoTrac's *Expanded Academic ASAP*.

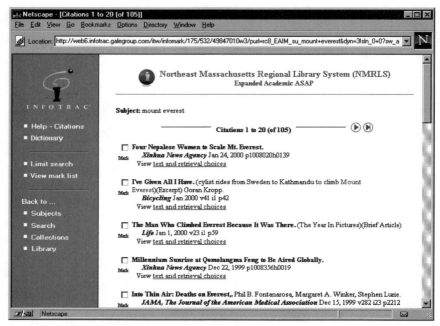

Figure 5.3: List of citations under the subject **Mount Everest** in InfoTrac's *Expanded Academic ASAP*.

is a reference to an article that provides all the information you need to locate that article.

The third article is "The Man Who Climbed Everest Because It Was There" which appeared in the January 2000 issue of *Life*. No author is cited. The citation goes on to give you the volume and issue numbers—in this case: volume 23, issue one. The volume number generally corresponds to the year of publication. *Life* has been published for 23 years (in its current monthly format, not the older weekly). This is the first issue of the year. The article starts on page 59.

Below the citation is a link to "View text." Just click here to see the complete text of the article. Although for this particular topic the first few articles are available, this index does not always provide the complete text. We just got lucky.

Most electronic indexes are limited in their full-text availability. Some publications don't want to have their material available electronically. Sometimes you'll see a citation in InfoTrac, for example, that simply says, "View extended citation" or "View abstract." An extended citation is just a citation that includes a bit more information than given in the brief format; an abstract is a summary of the article. Since these may still be excellent sources, check to see if your library subscribes to the periodical cited. You don't have to limit yourself to the articles that are available online.

This search was rather broad and found over one hundred articles. If you wanted a narrower list of articles, you could click on the option to "Narrow by subdivision" as displayed in Figure 5.2. The subdivisions of **Mount Everest** are shown in Figure 5.4.

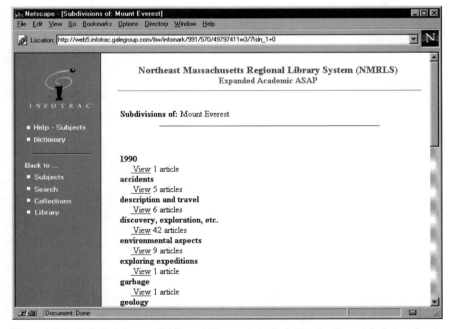

Figure 5.4: Subdivisions of **Mount Everest** in InfoTrac's *Expanded Academic ASAP*.

Each subheading has a smaller number of articles. You can view one article about Mount Everest in 1990, five articles about accidents on the mountain, six describing the place and travel, a larger group of 42 which focus on discovery and exploration, etc.

Just as most electronic indexes have a structure very similar to InfoTrac's *Expanded Academic ASAP*, you may also recognize similarities to the structure of online catalogs discussed in Chapter 2. As with online catalogs, you will often see cross-references to aid you in your subject searching. This example was a very easy search focusing on a concrete topic. Things are not always so simple. For this reason, electronic indexes have more advanced capabilities involving keyword searching and limiting, which I will discuss in Chapter 7. In the end, however, what you get is a list of citations, some of which will provide you with the text of the articles.

Print Indexes

Despite the prevalence of electronic indexes, I consider it important to understand how traditional print indexes are used for three reasons:

- Some indexes still have no computerized equivalents.
- It's always good to have a reliable backup if the computers go down in your library or if it's so busy at the end of the semester that you can't get time on a computer.
- The most important reason—if you want to find articles published before 1980, you will often need to use a print index. You may also need to use print indexes for articles published during the 1980s. Although there is some retrospective coverage, most electronic indexes only cover periodicals dating from the early 1990s (when online indexes emerged into widespread usage) to the present.

EVEREST, Mount

Assault on Everest. Newsweek 41:86 My 25 '53

By camera to the top. il Newsweek 43:54 Ja 25 '54

Commando tactics challenge Everest. G. Soule, il Pop Sci 162:105-7 My '53

Conquest of Everest. Time 62:24-6 Jl 6 '53

Conquest of Everest. il Life 34:18-25 Je 29 '53

Conquest of Everest, by J. Hunt. Review America 90:540 F 20 '54. P. Temple

Commentary 18:343-8 O '54. S. Marcus; Reply with rejoinder. J. Hunt. 18:475 N '54

New Repub 130:"17 F 1 '54. B. Bliven

Earth's third pole, Everest. M. Herzog. il N Y Times Mag p 12-13+ My 31 '53

Everest at last. Life 34:48 Je 15 '53

Figure 5.5: Listing of citations under the heading **Everest, Mount** in *Reader's Guide to Periodical Literature*.

What if you wanted to find articles written about the first successful climb to the top of Mount Everest in 1953 by Sir Edmund Hillary? You specifically want articles written at that time, not articles written more recently about that event. So electronic indexes that focus on the 1990s forward would be useless. Instead, go to a print index. *Reader's Guide to Periodical Literature* in book form was once *the* place to search for articles in popular magazines. Volumes of *Reader's Guide* go all the way back to 1900. It is now available in electronic form but shares the growing market with such online services as InfoTrac and EBSCOhost.

A print index like *Reader's Guide* consists of individual volumes that correspond to each year of periodicals covered. So, finding the volume for the time period you are interested in, look up **Mount Everest** in the alphabetically arranged *Reader's Guide*. You are referred to **EVEREST, Mount**. Under that heading you will see a listing of articles as displayed in figure 5.5.

As you can see from these citations, *Reader's Guide* covers only the most popular periodicals such as *Newsweek*, *Popular Science*, *Time*, *Life*, etc. The information given in these citations is basically the same as you would find in any electronic index except that the citations are a bit more abbreviated. The first article "Assault on Everest" appeared in *Newsweek* (volume 41, issue number 86) on May 25, 1953. The second article, "By Camera to the Top," includes pictures (that's what the abbreviation **il** indicates).

Reader's Guide often includes cross-references just as in an online catalog. Under many subject headings you will come across *see* and *see also* notations. This is helpful since the difficult aspect of using a print index is finding the proper subject heading. This is particularly true when looking up a more complex topic. Although the search for Mount Everest is deceptively easy, you will often find that your subject cannot be defined by a single heading and that you must skim through many irrelevant articles under a broad heading in order to find the specific one that you need. Once again, this is why electronic indexes are such an improvement over the print versions.

Index Selection

There are a wide variety of indexes focusing on particular fields of interest. The next chapter will introduce you to many of them. Just as you don't usually rely on a world atlas when taking a road trip but instead use a road map of the specific area of the country you're traveling in, you don't use *Expanded Academic ASAP* or *Reader's Guide* for every topic. Since many topics are interdisciplinary in nature, you can certainly find articles in more than one index.

For example, if you were doing a paper about the geology of Mount Everest, you might also want to consult a resource like *General Science Index*. To find articles about the tourism industry in Nepal and the growing interest in commercial expeditions to the summit of Mount Everest, you could take a look in a business index like InfoTrac's *Business ASAP*. *Biography Index* would provide citations to material about famous climbers of the world's highest mountain. You could also use a newspaper index like the *New York Times Index* to find newspaper articles.

When selecting which index to use, first become familiar with which ones are available at your library. Then consider the following:

- What is the subject focus of the index? Choose an index which pertains to the subject area for your topic. As the previous example demonstrates, you don't have to limit yourself to one single index.
- What type of material does it cover? Scholarly journals, trade journals, general magazines, newspapers, or a mixture? Your decision to use or not use a particular index will depend on your needs.
- What years are indexed? Be aware of what general time period is covered by the index. As explained before, you wouldn't want to search an electronic index that only includes citations for journal articles published in the 1990s if what you really want are articles published in the 1950s.

GETTING YOUR HANDS ON THE ARTICLES

So once you know where to go, how do you actually get there? In other words, once you have citations, how do you get your hands on the articles? If you've used an electronic index, you may have been able to retrieve the full text online. Still, electronic indexes provide many citations without the text. Don't pass these by just because you have to do some extra work. If you've used a print index, you'll definitely have to track down the articles. Since every library is arranged a bit differently, the paths will be somewhat varied, but I'll try to give you a general idea of how to arrive at your destination in the sometimes confusing land of periodicals.

Formats

You will find articles in three basic formats: hard copy, microfilm, and electronic. While hard copies are the actual physical magazines, newspapers, or journals, microfilm provides a space-saving copy on film that can be read and reproduced by using a microfilm machine. Believe it or not, at one time, microfilm was considered the latest in information technology, since a whole month's worth of newspapers or a year's worth of magazine issues could fit on one tiny roll of film. Today, microfilm seems outdated, awkward, and simply a pain to use. Still, it is common in many libraries and will be around for some time to come. Technically, *microfilm* is a type of *microform*; the other is *microfiche*, which comes in the form of cards.

Electronic indexes often provide text right on the screen, and sometimes graphics too. Increasingly, you can even view an exact replica of the article which, when printed out, looks like a photocopy of the actual article. In addition to printing out the article, most online indexes enable you to e-mail the article to yourself, or to download it to a disk. These two options help to save money and paper. Although some periodicals have their own Websites that might provide selected articles for free from current issues and maybe even selected ones from older issues, to access the full "archives" you usually have to be a subscriber. And searching through these individual Websites can be just as inefficient as browsing through hard copy issues of periodicals.

You may be tempted to use only those articles that are readily available online so that you can avoid using microfilm or having to track down the hard copy in the periodical room. By disregarding any index citations that might send you to the microfilm or periodical room, however, you may miss out on the most helpful information for your paper. You should not judge a periodical source by its format, but rather by its content. In the end, you'll be better off because having better sources makes it easier to write your research paper.

Periodical Organization

While the non-electronic copies of older magazines and newspapers are generally stored on microfilm, past issues of scholarly journals are often in book form, a year's worth of issues bound into a single volume. Not all libraries organize their periodicals in the same way. In some libraries, periodicals (both hard copy and microfilm) are arranged alphabetically by title. In other libraries, each periodical may be assigned a call number depending on its subject focus. All the same rules of Library of Congress or Dewey Decimal call numbers then apply. Bound volumes of journals arranged by call number may be shelved in the periodical room or in the same stacks where circulating books are found. Your library may even have closed stacks so that you must request the material and don't have to worry about how it is arranged. Familiarize yourself with the method of organization used to arrange periodicals in your library. Don't hesitate to ask a librarian for help if you can't easily determine the organizational scheme yourself.

What If Your Library Doesn't Have It?

There are tens of thousands of magazines and journals being published in the world today, along with thousands of newspapers. With so many periodicals available, not every library can subscribe to every one, so academic libraries generally subscribe to what are known as the core (or most important) journals in those fields in which the college specializes. They may also get some of the peripheral (or less essential) journals in these same fields as well as many general magazines, major newspapers like the *New York*

Times, and the local papers for the area in which the library is located. Your library should have some sort of a list of all its subscriptions either on paper or on its Website. You may also be able to search for a periodical title in the same way you look for a book title in the online catalog.

If your library doesn't subscribe to the periodical you need to complete your paper or have it available in electronic format through a full-text index, don't lose hope. If you have allotted yourself sufficient time for obstacles along the way (as I advised you to do in the beginning of this book), you can take advantage of the resources of other libraries.

A librarian can help you determine whether a periodical is in another library in your area. If the library is part of a consortium, there may be a list of the holdings of the other member libraries available. You can then either go to the library yourself to copy the article (since most periodicals don't circulate) or you may even be able to have a copy sent to your own library.

If the periodical cannot be located in the immediate vicinity, your library can obtain it through interlibrary loan (ILL). Even if the article you need is in an obscure scholarly journal held by only a handful of libraries in the country, your library's ILL department can request this article and usually get it to you within a week or two. The time factor involved here is the main drawback of ILL and the reason that many students, starting their papers too late, cannot take advantage of this valuable service.

Finding articles is an essential part of your research. For some narrow or very recent topics, as I mentioned previously, articles may provide you with the only information you can find. So don't get lost and frustrated. Keep going in the right direction by using the appropriate periodical indexes.

Six

Modes of Transportation, Part I:
Choosing Electronic Resources

Just as there are many makes and models of cars and the decision about which one to buy is often a difficult one, the range of electronic resources available in your library or through your library's Website is sometimes overwhelming. How do you know which databases to use? Fortunately, you don't have to pick just one, and you also don't have to spend any money. But you can sure waste a lot of time if you use an inappropriate resource; you may never even find the information you need. This chapter will make sense of the ever-expanding variety of electronic databases and give you the background you need to feel comfortable selecting the right ones. It will focus on the content of computerized resources, enabling you to choose wisely, while the next chapter will focus on using these resources, building upon the fundamentals of how to search an online catalog discussed in Chapter 2.

TYPES OF ACCESS

There are two main ways of accessing electronic resources: on CD-ROM and online. CD-ROMs are discs that can store a huge amount of data in the form of text as well as graphics, animation, and video (in case you're curious, ROM stands for "read only memory," which basically means that once data is encoded on the disc, it can't be altered, only read). An entire encyclopedia can fit on a single disc; so can a periodical index containing citations for an entire decade of articles. If you search the disc properly, you can quickly find any piece of information stored on it. In general, CD-ROMs can only be used within the library. Many CD-ROM databases have been replaced by online versions, but you still find this format in just about all libraries because some databases are only available on CD-ROM; it can also be a more economical way for a library to provide a resource than online. Another advantage of CD-ROMs is that they can work more quickly than an online database—you don't get caught in the "heavy traffic" caused by many people being on the computer network at the same time. But CD-ROMs have limitations; even with their large storage capacity, databases—especially ones that provide the full text of articles—are becoming too large to fit on a single disc. It's also harder to update a CD-ROM. Online databases tend to have more recent information because they can be updated at a central location whereas an updated CD-ROM has to be produced and then sent to a library, which must then install the new disc.

The other means by which you gain access to electronic databases is online. Today, this generally means via the World Wide Web. Access is usually restricted to these Web databases. Sometimes you can only use them within the library, or you may be able to get to them from the library's homepage in your dorm room or at any computer on campus. Another way of restricting access is to implement passwords (often your student ID number) so you can use the resources from virtually any location.

The cost and quality of the online databases I will highlight here differentiate them from the free Web sources that I will discuss in Chapter 8. In other words, when you search a Web-based periodical index or reference source, you are generally using a resource that has undergone a rigorous editorial process that enhances its quality and accuracy. Your library pays for the database and access is limited. There are exceptions, however. For example, governmental Websites are excellent sources of authoritative information and many are now freely accessible on the Web. There are also some sites that provide free access to the indexing of articles but charge a fee for the full text. Usually, if a database is available for free on the Web, it is because the producer accepts advertising. Intrusive banner ads at the top of the screen and annoying pop-up ads degrade a resource intended for academic research (in my humble opinion).

BENEFITS OF ELECTRONIC RESOURCES

Both online and CD-ROM resources share many advantages over traditional resources in print:

- Since multiple volumes of an index, an encyclopedia, or some other type of reference source can be stored in a single database, you save all the time it would take you to repeat your search in each volume of a print source.
- Computerized indexes take up a lot less physical space than books, so it is possible to include abstracts for each citation.
- You don't have to copy citations by hand or make poor quality photocopies; instead, you can print out any pertinent information that you find; you can also download to a disk, and, in some cases, e-mail records to yourself.
- It's also much easier to search a computerized resource because you can use keywords.

TYPES OF DATABASES

There are four main types of electronic databases used in libraries:

- Bibliographic—these are indexes providing citations to articles and perhaps abstracts but no complete text.
- Full-text—indexes that provide the text of articles or reference sources, such as encyclopedias, which include the complete textual content of the print version. Some common full-text reference databases are *Encyclopedia of Associations*, *Current Biography*, and *Facts On File World News Digest*.
- Full-image—these databases provide an exact replica of the print version; for instance, InfoTrac's *Expanded Academic ASAP* is partially a full-image database because it includes copies of some articles that, when printed out, look even better than photocopied versions of the same articles from the hard copies of the periodicals.
- Multimedia—these resources combine text and graphics with animation, video, and/or sound. For example, *Grolier's Multimedia Encyclopedia* contains all twenty-one volumes of the text of the *Academic American Encyclopedia* as well as pictures, maps, animation, video, and sound. You can look up "John Kennedy," for instance, and, in addition to reading about him, watch video clips from his most famous speeches.

Sometimes these types of databases overlap in a single resource. A database may provide bibliographic citations for some articles, full text for others, and complete images for others.

POPULAR ELECTRONIC RESOURCES

For the next few pages, I will describe in greater detail the most popular online services in libraries, and the databases they provide. As with the reference sources I described in Chapter 4, not every library will have every one, but you should be able to access at least a few; if not, you might want to consult another library in your area. Before proceeding, it is important to understand that an online service usually provides access to a number of different subject-specific databases. InfoTrac, for example, is not one particular database, but the name of a service that includes a variety of resources. Think of an online service like a car dealership; the individual databases provided are like the different car models. If you go to a Toyota dealer, you don't ask to see a Toyota; instead, you probably have specific models in mind, like a Corolla, Tercel, or Camry. In the same way, when you use InfoTrac or one of the other online services, you need to select a specific database to search. The majority of databases available are periodical indexes, but there are also a wide variety of online reference sources.

I don't want to get too bogged down in details like how many periodicals each database indexes, how much full-text coverage is provided, or what years are included. I started to do this and realized that all the descriptions began to sound the same: "hundreds (maybe thousands) of periodicals indexed, text available for a large percentage, and coverage generally for the past ten years or so." Besides, these descriptions are constantly changing and you won't remember them anyway. Instead, I want to give you a sense of the subject focus of each source since that's what matters most when deciding which ones to use.

Among different databases and database providers there is often overlap in what information is covered. An index like InfoTrac's *Expanded Academic ASAP*, for example, covers many of the same periodicals as EBSCOhost's *Academic Search Elite*, but there are certain titles that are unique to each of these databases. To offer another metaphor, it's like shopping in a mall. Similar types of stores will carry a lot of the same merchandise. But, if one store doesn't have exactly what you want, you simply go to another. The bottom line is that there is no single source to consult when researching your topic. You may have to go through a process of trial and error and search more than one database. It's okay to search multiple databases; what you want to avoid is wasting your time searching a database that is inappropriate.

You will also find that some of the same databases are available through different online services. For example, an index to educational materials called *ERIC*, which is produced by the United States government, is accessible through EBSCOhost, SilverPlatter, and FirstSearch. Online services don't have to actually produce the databases included in their collections, although some do. The primary purpose of the online services we will look at is to provide access to databases. One online service that will be highlighted in this chapter, SilverPlatter, produces no original material at all, but provides access to hundreds of resources produced by other companies.

InfoTrac

Gale Group produces InfoTrac databases. *Expanded Academic ASAP*, which we saw in the last chapter, is part of the InfoTrac collection of resources. Although the InfoTrac databases are also available on CD-ROM, an increasingly common way of accessing them is through InfoTrac Web, which indexes more titles and provides more full-text coverage. *Expanded Academic ASAP* is a very popular resource in academic libraries because it covers a wide selection of scholarly journals.

Other InfoTrac databases you are likely to encounter include:

- *General Periodicals ASAP*—this index focuses on more popular general interest publications.
- *Business ASAP*, *General BusinessFile ASAP*, *Predicasts PROMT*, and *F&S Index*—all of these sources index business magazines and trade journals.
- *Health Reference Center*—this index covers medical and general health topics.
- *Contemporary Authors*—this is not an index but a full-text reference source that provides biographical sketches for just about any writer you can think of who is currently living or who died after 1960.

Simply stated, if your library has InfoTrac, it is one of the best places to start with your research, and, in general, *Expanded Academic ASAP* is the most appropriate database to use for finding academic material.

EBSCOhost

EBSCOhost is very similar to InfoTrac. This service provides access to a number of resources including the *Academic Search* databases, which are similar *to Expanded Academic ASAP* in content, covering a wide variety of subject areas. Your library might subscribe to the *Elite, Select,* or *Plus* editions, which differ only in the number of full-text titles provided. Among the other indexes that EBSCOhost produces are:

- *MasterFile*—for popular magazines.
- *Business Source*—covers business magazines, trade, and academic journals.
- *Newspaper Source*—besides indexing articles in leading national newspapers like *The New York Times*, *The Wall Street Journal, USA Today*, and *The Christian Science Monitor*, the text of over a hundred local, regional, and international papers is included, as well as newswires such as the Associated Press.

Figure 6.1: Opening search screen for EBSCOhost's *Academic Search Elite*.

In addition to the indexes that it produces, EBSCOhost also provides access to many resources produced by other companies. Your library will probably not subscribe to all of these, but you might see such reference sources as *Facts On File World News Digest*, *Funk & Wagnalls New Encyclopedia*, or *Hoover's Company Profiles* and such indexes as *ERIC* and *Medline*.

ProQuest

ProQuest databases are noted for being among the first to provide not just the full text but also the page images for periodicals covered by its indexes. Although access is provided through ProQuest, you will also see these databases in FirstSearch, which will be described further along. Among the popular ProQuest databases are:

- *Periodical Abstracts* and *General Periodicals*—these indexes both provide broad coverage of popular as well as academic periodicals. While *Periodical Abstracts*, as its title implies, only gives abstracts of the articles indexed (unless you have access to the *PlusText* edition), full text is available for many articles via *General Periodicals*.

- *Newspaper Abstracts*—this resource indexes and abstracts the leading national and regional newspapers, including *The New York Times* and *The Wall Street Journal*. Your library might also subscribe to the separate ProQuest database, which provides the complete text of *The New York Times* back to 1981.
- *Business Periodicals* and *ABI/Inform*—these indexes provide abstracts for business and management journals, including many international journals.

H.W. Wilson

The most well-known Wilson index is *The Reader's Guide to Periodical Literature*, which has been available in print since 1900. The H.W. Wilson Company has published subject-specific indexes for years, but, in keeping up with the times, now also produces electronic versions of its popular indexes both online and on CD-ROM. These indexes have the added feature of abstracts. Recently, Wilson has extended the coverage of its online products to include older material so, if your library subscribes, you may not have to use the print indexes at all. Wilson has their own online service, WilsonWeb, but also makes their databases available through FirstSearch and SilverPlatter.

Wilson indexes are very subject-specific as indicated by the titles below. Most of these databases are available in versions that provide abstracts and/or text.

- *Applied Science & Technology Index*—covers subjects relating to practical applications of science including engineering, computers, telecommunications, transportation, and waste management.

Figure 6.2: Opening search screen for *Art Index* via WilsonWeb.

- *Art Index*—coverage of fine arts.
- *Biography Index*—covers periodicals as well as books that contain information about famous people. Wilson also publishes numerous biographical reference sources itself, including *Current Biography* and *World Authors 800 BC to Present*, available in print and electronically. A new database, *Wilson Biographies*, combines the information from all of their biographical sources into one database.
- *Book Review Digest*—includes excerpts from book reviews in popular review sources.
- *Business Periodicals Index*—also *Wilson Business Abstracts* and *Wilson Business Full Text*.
- *Education Index*—as the title implies, covers topics relating to education.
- *General Science Index*—covers articles on pure science (as opposed to applied science).
- *Humanities Index*—covers a variety of subjects includ-

ing literature and language, history, philosophy, archaeology, classics, performing arts, history, and religion.
- *Reader's Guide Abstracts*—the "classic" index; a full-
text version is also available.
- *Social Sciences Index*—coverage includes such topics
as anthropology, area studies, economics, political science, psychiatry, psychology, social work and public
welfare, sociology, urban studies, women's studies, etc.

Wilson also produces *OmniFile*. The *OmniFile Mega Edition* basically combines the education, general science, humanities, and social sciences indexes along with *Wilson
Business Full Text* and *Reader's Guide*.

FirstSearch

FirstSearch, produced by an organization called OCLC, is
yet another collection of databases; but it is more extensive
than most, currently giving library users access to 85 resources. This collection includes all of the Wilson indexes,
and other popular indexes such as *ERIC*, *Medline*, and the
GPO Monthly Catalog. Many reference sources are also provided, such as the *World Book Electronic Encyclopedia*,
Facts On File World News Digest, and *Disclosure*, which
provides financial reports.

OCLC also produces some of its own databases, among
them:

- *WorldCat*—this is like an online book catalog for the
entire world! With one search you can search online
catalogs worldwide.
- *NetFirst*—provides citations for Websites on a vast ar-
ray of topics as well as direct links to these sites. Because the sites included are evaluated for quality, this
database can be much more useful than the free Web
search engines that usually retrieve irrelevant and low-
quality resources.
- *ArticleFirst* and *ContentsFirst*—two good databases for

Figure 6.3: Opening screen for OCLC's FirstSearch.

finding articles on a broad range of topics in both popular and academic sources.

SilverPlatter

SilverPlatter does not produce any of its own content, but
they provide access to over two hundred databases produced
by other companies, like Wilson, utilizing the SilverPlatter
Information Retrieval System (SPIRS) displayed in Figure
6.4. Their databases are available in both CD-ROM and
online formats. Among the more popular databases provided
to libraries by SilverPlatter are *PsycINFO*, *ERIC*, and
Medline. The company also provides access to such reference sources as *Contemporary Authors*, *Encyclopedia of
Associations*, and *Who's Who*.

© 1967–2000 American Psychological Association
© 1990–2000 SilverPlatter International N.V.

Figure 6.4: Opening search screen for SilverPlatter's *PsycINFO*.

LEXIS-NEXIS' *Academic Universe*

Always popular in newsrooms and corporate libraries, LEXIS-NEXIS used to be a rare find in academic libraries except for large research institutions. But a new service called *Academic Universe* is specifically geared towards the college market. Best known for its full-text coverage and current information on business, legal, and news topics, the emphasis of LEXIS-NEXIS is not on scholarly research. Instead, it provides access to thousands of sources, including newspapers and magazines, world news services, newswire services, television transcripts, SEC filings, and federal and state laws and regulations. Many sources are updated daily.

Figure 6.5: Homepage of LEXIS-NEXIS' *Academic Universe.*

Dialog@CARL

Dialog is an online database service that has been around for a long time but until recently was not available to students. Since this extensive collection of highly specialized databases was very complicated and expensive to use, you usually had to have a librarian search it for you. Dialog was only available as a service for professionals in corporate and academic libraries rather than for library users. But now the Dialog@CARL version of this service, which is produced by the CARL Corporation, is available—think of it as "Dialog Lite." As a select group of about three hundred Dialog databases accessible in a Web-based format, Dialog@CARL is user-friendly enough for anyone to search.

Dialog@CARL should not be your first stop—it's more like the "end of the road." Many of the databases are very specific; for instance, the full text of individual newspapers

Figure 6.6: Homepage for Dialog@CARL.

not found elsewhere, like the *Anchorage Daily News* and the *South China Morning Post*, reference resources such as the *American Library Directory*, and extremely narrow indexes like *World Surface Coatings Abstracts*. If your library provides access to Dialog@CARL and you haven't found what you need using the other online services available, see what it has to offer.

"Free" Websites Worthy of Mention

So far, all of the resources I have listed will only be available to you if your library subscribes to them. Because they are not free databases, they are generally of a higher quality than most of the free resources you will find on the Web. "You get what you pay for," as they say. There are a few resources, however, available to anyone with access to the Web that fall into the scope of this chapter. One such category is governmental information. The other includes Websites that index periodicals for free but charge a fee for the full text.

United States Government Databases

The United States government is one of the most prolific publishers in the world. Some of the popular databases already mentioned in this chapter are compiled by governmental agencies. For example, *Medline* is the National Library of Medicine's database to more than eleven million articles published in over four thousand medical journals. Although it is one of the resources available via EBSCOhost, FirstSearch, SilverPlatter, and other services, you can also access it for free by going to *www.nlm.nih.gov.*

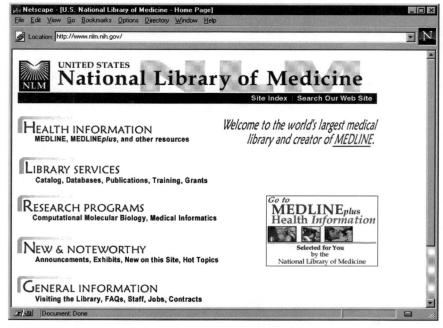

Figure 6.7: The National Library of Medicine's homepage providing free access to *Medline.*

ERIC is another database offered by various online services that can also be accessed at a governmental Website. *ERIC*, which stands for Educational Resources Information Center, is supported by the U.S. Department of Education, the Office of Educational Research and Improvement, and the National Library of Education, and provides access to abstracts of almost one million documents and journal articles concerning educational topics. It is available at *www.accesseric.org.*

Another important resource is the *GPO Monthly Catalog*, also known as the *Catalog of United States Government Publications*, which indexes the publications of the Government Printing Office (GPO). While some of the publications indexed are available online, all can be obtained at any one of the numerous Federal Depository libraries throughout the

Figure 6.8: The Educational Resources Information Center (*ERIC*) homepage.

Figure 6.9: GPO Access database list.

country. To use this catalog, go to the GPO Access database list at *www.access.gpo.gov/su_docs/db2.html*, where you will also find a list of other governmental databases available, ranging from the complete *Budget of the United States Government* to the *Weekly Compilation of Presidential Documents.*

You may be wondering why your library would provide access to these databases through subscription-based services if they're available for free. When a database is available from different online services, the way in which you use the database differs depending on what service you are using. So if you're accustomed to searching EBSCOhost databases it might be easier for you to search *ERIC* via EBSCOhost than to struggle with an unfamiliar user interface.

CARL UnCover

Website address: *http://uncweb.carl.org*

The *UnCover* database available from the CARL Corporation indexes over 18,000 periodicals. While it is freely available to anyone with access to the Web, acquiring the text of the articles entails a fee. Over eight million articles written since fall 1988 can be faxed; some can even be sent via e-mail. If you don't have time for interlibrary loan or to go to another library and you desperately need an article, *UnCover* is a good "last resort." The fees, however, can be somewhat hefty for college students struggling to pay for pizza and gas, not to mention textbooks.

Northern Light

Northern Light is a Web search engine. The reason I highlight it here rather than in the upcoming chapter on searching the Web is because it offers a unique feature—in addition to searching for Websites, Northern Light also searches its "Special Collection" of over five thousand periodicals. Even if your library subscribes to no other electronic indexes (which is unlikely in this day and age), or for some reason you are unable to access your library's resources, you can go to Northern Light as long as you can get on the Web. Searching Northern Light is free, but to obtain the full text of the Special Collection articles indexed you must pay a fee. In most cases, the cost is very modest compared to a database like UnCover.

Figure 6.10: Northern Light's homepage at *www.northernlight.com.*

OK—that's enough! Your head must be spinning. There are certainly other databases that I have not covered here, but this book is not intended to turn you into a librarian. Being familiar with the major online services you are likely to encounter is sufficient and can help you understand the other lesser-known ones that may also be available in your library. Just as there are many different modes of transportation (cars, trucks, buses, trains, motorcycles, SUVs, etc.), there are different resources for different research topics. Each serves a purpose, and each must be chosen with your particular needs in mind.

Seven

Modes of Transportation, Part II:
Using Electronic Resources

Now that you're familiar with the different "makes" and "models" of databases, it's time to start the engine and take a test drive. Many of the principles explained in Chapter 2 apply here because an online book catalog is basically just another kind of database. And you already know the basics of searching computerized indexes from Chapter 5. Most students never get beyond the basic search screens and simple keyword searching. They just accept the results they get and make the best of it. But advanced searching allows you to really focus in on your topic. It's like taking a good photograph. First, you have to look through the viewfinder and get just the right angle; then you have to bring the picture into focus. So don't settle in a figurative way for fuzzy, off-center snapshots.

In this chapter, we will focus on some more advanced searching techniques, while also reviewing some of the principles already discussed and how they can be applied to a variety of resources. Although the emphasis of this chapter will be on indexes, many of the principles apply to any type of searchable database, including the World Wide Web.

ACCESSING DATABASES

Before you can search a database for information, you must be able to access it. So the first step in using database resources is to find out which ones you have at your disposal. In many cases, you can just go to your library's Website and see what's available. Often there will be a link on the homepage to the part of the site that lists the individual online databases that the library subscribes to. This link may be called a variety of things: "electronic resources," "online databases," "computerized indexes," etc. If your library doesn't have too many resources, the databases may all be listed on the homepage. Library Websites are as unique as each library, so if you have any problems navigating, consult a librarian. Remember, however, that some databases may only be accessible on-campus even if there are links to them; others may require you to enter a password. Also be aware that CD-ROMs and online resources that are not Web-based may only be available for use within the library.

Most online services provide a number of databases. EBSCOhost and InfoTrac list all their resources on a single Web page, while LEXIS-NEXIS' *Academic Universe*, Dialog@CARL, and FirstSearch offer so many databases that there is usually an intermediate screen which divides the sources by subject. Referring back to Figure 6.5, for example, you can see that LEXIS-NEXIS divides its databases into the following categories: News, Business, Legal Research, Medical, and Reference. Click on "News" and you will see the screen displayed in Figure 7.1, which provides links to all the news-related databases.

Since Dialog@CARL provides over three hundred databases, it hierarchically divides them into seventeen subject areas. In addition to areas relating to law, medicine, and business, Dialog has such categories as Humanities and Arts, Sciences, and Technology and Engineering. There is overlap among these subjects because some Dialog databases fit into more than one category.

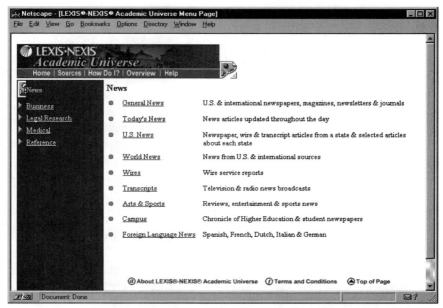

Figure 7.1: Databases available via LEXIS-NEXIS' *Academic Universe* in the "News" category.

Some online services allow you to search in more than one database at a time. Dialog@CARL lets you select up to six databases to search simultaneously. FirstSearch helps you select the most appropriate databases by allowing you to do a broad search in a number of files; you are then given the estimated number of results so you can choose the databases that come up with the most information. In EBSCOhost, you simply check off all the sources that you want to search on the initial listing. So, if *Academic Search* and *MasterFile* are both relevant to your research you may want to search them together.

SEARCHING DATABASES

Once you access your database (or databases), it's time to search. This section will outline many of the features common to all databases, including a review of some of the principles discussed in Chapter 2. Although you may want to find articles written by the same author or an article with a particular title, the most frequent way of searching an electronic index is by subject or keyword. There is also an emerging method known as natural language searching that is really just a variation on keyword searching.

Subject vs. Keyword Searching

There are no standard subject headings used to classify articles the way in which you have the *Library of Congress Subject Headings* for books. Each online service and sometimes even individual databases have their own terminology. This can make subject searching, except for simple topics, somewhat difficult. Some databases even have special names for the subject-heading field: *PsycINFO* has descriptors and *Medline* has MESHs (medical subject headings).

A good example of the inconsistency of subject headings is provided by the cover story from the August 1999 *U.S. News & World Report* entitled "Schools Turn Off the Tap" that concerns steps being taken by colleges to curtail binge drinking. Notice the comparison between the headings given to the same article in two different databases.

In EBSCOhost's *Academic Search*:

**drinking of alcoholic beverages—universities and
   colleges
universities and colleges—social life and customs
college students—alcohol use**

In InfoTrac's *Expanded Academic ASAP*:

**alcohol—usage
fraternal organizations—social aspects
universities and colleges—alcohol use**

Because of these inconsistencies, I suggest you start with keyword searching unless your topic is very straightforward. If you're looking for articles about a certain person or place, for example, there are usually not many variations. You can also enter a broad topic and then browse through the subheadings for that subject.

As with searching for books, determining the appropriate subject headings is still the best way to get a comprehensive listing of very relevant articles. Keyword searching presents the problems of finding irrelevant material and/or not finding all the relevant material. But even if you find just one really good article through keyword searching, you can take a look at the subject headings given the article and backtrack, clicking on an appropriate heading. For example, let's say you wanted to find articles about binge drinking on college campuses. If you enter **college campuses and binge**

Figure 7.2: Records retrieved in EBSCOhost's *Academic Search* for a search on **college campuses and binge drinking**.

drinking as your keyword search in EBSCOhost's *Academic Search*, seven records are retrieved, as displayed in Figure 7.2.

The first is titled "Social Marketing Program Slows Binge Drinking On College Campuses." You retrieve that citation and view the record shown in Figure 7.3.

Notice the subject headings for this article. **COLLEGE students—Alcohol use—United States** sounds like a relevant subject. Since this heading is actually a Web link, you can click on it and retrieve all the articles on that subject. By doing this, you come up with a much larger set of 82 articles. So always look at the headings of appropriate articles. They could lead you to a gold mine of related information.

Figure 7.3: Full record for an article in EBSCOhost *Academic Search*.

Natural Language Searching

Natural language searching is a new method of searching in which you simply type in a question as you would ask it. For example: "What are the effects of television violence on children?" Although this might make you feel uncomfortable, as if you are communicating with a computer that has a personality and a brain like Hal in the movie *2001*, what is actually happening is quite simple: the computer ignores any superfluous words and does a keyword search for all the significant words. In the above example, the computer would do a search for "effects," "television," "violence," and "children." Usually, the connector OR is implied between terms and the resultant set of records, which can be quite large, is sorted in order of relevancy so that the records containing the highest occurrence of the search words are at the top of the list. This can be a somewhat imprecise method of searching that may work well for some topics but often retrieves irrelevant results for others.

Broadening Your Search

Searching the Full Text

If you haven't found many articles and need more information, you can broaden your search in many databases by searching the complete text of available articles. Most databases automatically limit their searches to the citation and abstract. Be forewarned, however, that full-text searching increases your chances of finding irrelevant material much more so than when only the abstract is searched. One of your search terms may only be mentioned in passing and have very little to do with the main focus of the article. An article about fraternities, for example, might mention binge drinking, while the article is really about the history of fraternities.

Figure 7.4: InfoTrac's keyword search mode.

If you look at the opening search screen for EBSCOhost in the last chapter (Figure 6.1), you will see that you can click on the option "search within full text articles" on the right side of the screen. In InfoTrac's keyword search mode, as displayed in Figure 7.4, the default is searching "in title, citation, abstract" but you can change this to "in entire article content."

Using OR and Truncation

Since Boolean searching is applicable in just about any searchable database, another way of expanding your search is to think of synonyms for your terms and link them with the connector OR, which, as you'll recall, searches for any of the terms entered. You will either have to type in the word OR between terms or, in some databases, select it from a pull-down menu. Truncation is a variation on this method. By entering the appropriate symbol at the end of a word, all variant endings will be found. Because this symbol differs, and in some databases variant endings are searched for automatically, you should refer to the "help" section of the database to find out what to do (most databases provide in-depth instructions on truncation and many other features—just look for the word "help" on the screen and click it).

Narrowing Your Search

Using Limiters

You can also limit your search in very specific ways if you have found too much. The following are limiters that are commonly available in many databases:

- Limiting by Periodical—You might have a specific journal in mind; most databases allow you to search a single periodical. This is extremely narrow, however. Before doing this, you will want to find out if the database does, indeed, index the source you are interested in. You can usually find a list of the sources covered online. In EBSCOhost, for example, there is a "Journal Search" button to click on the top of the page.
- Limiting by Date—There is often the option of searching only a certain date or range of dates.
- Limiting to Articles with Full Text—In databases that contain the complete text for only selected articles, you can limit your results by searching for only the citations that also have the text. Even though this makes things easier for you, however, just be aware that you might be missing some wonderful sources.
- Limiting to Peer-Reviewed Journals—A limiter available in a number of databases that index academic journals, including *Expanded Academic ASAP* and *Academic Search*, is limiting to "peer-reviewed" publications. This search will only find articles in scholarly journals that are refereed, meaning that an article

must be accepted for publication by a group of scholars.

If you refer back to Figure 7.4, you can see the limiters
available in InfoTrac. To limit by periodical, you enter a title;
to limit by date you enter it in the box provided; and to limit
to full-text or peer-reviewed publications, you simply click
the appropriate boxes.

Using AND and NOT

You can also narrow your search by using the Boolean connectors AND or NOT. Just to review, connect terms with
AND if you want to find all of them or with NOT if you
want to exclude a term. In many databases, the term AND
is implied between terms; in others, you still have to enter
it or select it from a pull-down menu. To add to the confu-
sion, sometimes AND NOT or BUT NOT is used instead of
simply NOT. If the specifics of how to search a database are
not obvious on the search screen, they will probably be explained in greater detail in the "help" section.

Proximity Operators

In addition to Boolean connectors, you can also use something called a *proximity operator*, which allows you to narrow your search by specifying that two or more words
appear within a certain number of words of each other. Proximity operators are usually composed of the letter N for
"near" or W for "within" and then a number to specify the
number of words. You place the proximity operator between
the words that are to be searched. For example, **Television
N5 violence** in EBSCOhost will find "television violence"
as well as "violence in movies and television." **Television
w/5 violence** in LEXIS-NEXIS will do the same thing. Depending on what database you are in, however, word order
may be important. For instance, the word **television** might

have to be before **violence** in the example above. So once again, consult those "help" files to find out.

Field-Specific Searching

Just like a book record, any database record is composed of fields—the individual pieces of information that describe the item. In the case of a periodical article, these fields would include:

- author
- article title—or headline in the case of a newspaper article
- periodical title—this is sometimes referred to as the source
- subject headings—also commonly referred to as descriptors
- abstract—a summary of an article
- text—if available; some databases designate a separate field for the lead paragraph of an article. This is helpful for searching purposes because if your keywords appear in the first paragraph, it is likely that they are not just passing references; therefore the articles retrieved when searching the lead paragraph will be more relevant than those found searching the entire article.

Generally, when you do a basic keyword search, the entire citation and the abstract for each record in the database are searched automatically, even though the chances of retrieving irrelevant articles are increased if the abstracts are searched. Limiting your search to certain fields in the records can be very effective in focusing your search and reducing the number of irrelevant articles you find.

When you go to the advanced searching screen in InfoTrac, displayed in Figure 7.5, you will see a form that includes a pull-down menu. This menu lets you choose which "index" to search ("index" in this context means the same thing as "field"). You can choose the basic "keyword"

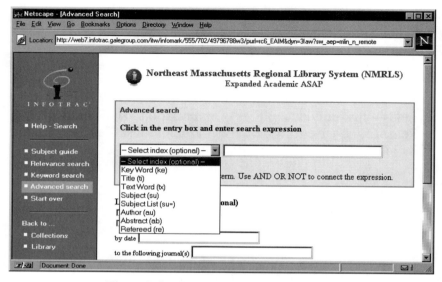

Figure 7.5: Advanced searching in InfoTrac.

that will do a standard search for your term in the citations and abstracts, or "title," which will only find those records that contain your term in the articles' titles. Another option is searching by "text word," which is the same as searching the complete text of the article for your terms.

There are two types of subject searches: either "subject (su)" or "subject list (su=)." The first type of search will retrieve any articles that have subject headings containing the search term specified, but not necessarily beginning with that term. "Subject list," on the other hand, will put you in the alphabetically arranged subject-heading list at the point you specify. To differentiate, let's say you entered **alcohol** as a subject search. This would find any article that contains the term **alcohol** in any of the subject headings. This would include articles with the heading **alcohol—usage** as well as **universities and colleges—alcohol use**. If you entered this same term as a subject list search, however, you would retrieve a list of subject headings beginning with the word **alcohol** that you could then select from to retrieve articles.

This can be helpful for cross-references. If you look up **ado-lescents** in the subject list, for example, you would be instructed to use **teenagers** instead, since this is the official heading. Many databases have this sort of feature—some call it a thesaurus. It's a way of determining what subject headings can be used. It's a bit like looking up Library of Congress headings in the "red books."

Finally, you can limit your search to the author field in the pull-down menu, or to the abstract. If you wanted to find all the articles indexed by *Expanded Academic ASAP* that were written by Carl Sagan, for example, you would go to the advanced search screen, select author from the pull-down menu, and then enter Carl Sagan and press "search."

Fields that can be searched differ in just about every database depending on what would be useful to the searcher. In the *General News* database in LEXIS-NEXIS' *Academic Universe*, the "More Options" form lets you search for words in the headline, the lead paragraph, the complete text, the caption, and the author. In *Business News*, you can search by company name or ticker symbol.

Combining Field-Specific Searches

If your topic is at all complex, you will benefit by combining a number of field-specific searches. Consider a topic like the abuse of drugs and alcohol among adolescents. Sure, you could do a keyword search for the main terms, but as I hope I have made clear, keyword searching is often inferior to subject searching. Because there is no single subject heading to define this topic, go to InfoTrac's advanced search screen. Figure 7.6 displays the search for this topic.

First, select the subject index (su) from the pull-down menu and enter **drugs or alcohol** as your search expression in the box. This will find any articles that have the terms **drugs** or **alcohol** anywhere in the subject-heading field. Remember, the subject headings don't actually have to start with these terms. This set (R1) contains a hefty and unman-

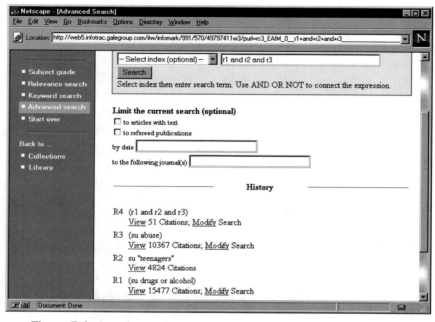

Figure 7.6: An advanced search for **drug and alcohol abuse among adolescents**.

ageable 15,477 articles. Next, look up **adolescents** in the subject list (su=) since you're not sure if this is a valid subject heading. Another screen pops up informing you that **teenagers** is the appropriate term to use; select that heading and you will be returned to the advanced search screen. **Teenagers** creates a second set, R2, with 4,824 citations. Then search for **abuse** in the subject index, which creates set R3 with 10,367 records. Now it's time to combine all the sets, creating a fourth set that contains only those records that have the terms **drugs** or **alcohol** and **abuse** somewhere in the subject headings, as well as the distinct subject heading **teenagers**. This resultant set is 51 highly relevant articles. Just about every database lets you perform a variation of this technique.

A REVIEW OF THE DIRECTIONS

Perhaps you're feeling a bit overwhelmed and slightly lost at this point, especially after my final example. That's okay. I told you that this chapter would cover some advanced searching techniques. I'll admit, what I've covered is a bit daunting, and I wouldn't expect you to remember how to do it all. It's beneficial just to be aware of what you could do. It's like cruise control in a car—you might never use it, but it's nice to have it anyway. In a nutshell, here are the main points you should remember:

- Find out what databases are available at your library (via your library's Website or ask a librarian). Choose the most appropriate database for your research needs; if you don't find enough in that database, you can always try another.
- If your topic is broad or straightforward, start with a subject search; otherwise try a basic keyword search. If you've found a manageable set of records (I prefer less than fifty), browse through the first screen of titles and check to see that most of them are relevant. Take a closer look at the full records for the items that sound best. If any subject heading looks particularly applicable, do a new search using this heading (often all you have to do is click on it).
- If you've come up with records that don't seem to be relevant, revise your search using different keywords and try again.
- If you haven't found enough records, broaden your search by
    - a) entering additional terms and connecting them with OR
    - b) using truncated terms
    - c) searching the full text of records, not just the citation and abstract.
- If you've found too many records, narrow your search by:

    a) using limiters to specify a certain periodical, date, etc.

    b) entering additional terms and connecting them with AND

    c) excluding a term using NOT.

- You can further refine your search by limiting it to certain fields in the record, and by combining two or more field-specific searches. This often requires you to go to an advanced search screen.

Unless you're really into cars, you don't know how to deal with every mechanical problem. But it's good to know some of the basics like changing a tire. In the same way, don't feel that you have to be an expert at searching every database. It's more practical to focus on one—preferably the one that will cover the majority of your research needs such as *Expanded Academic ASAP* or *Academic Search*. When the need arises for you to use another, more specific, database, you can always ask a librarian for help just as you can go to a mechanic when your car needs fixing.

Eight

Uncharted Territory:
The World Wide Web

Considering the metaphors I have used throughout this book, the cliché of the "information superhighway" is hard to avoid when discussing the World Wide Web. There are ways in which this image is accurate and other ways in which it seems completely wrong. The Web certainly has the potential to provide the user with a wealth of quick information, but the reality is that it also has road-blocks of its own. The attitude of this chapter is, therefore, "proceed with caution." Don't rely on the Web alone for your research paper.

This chapter will only provide a brief introduction to the immensity of the World Wide Web. Entire books have been written about how to use the Web. These books quickly go out-of-date because the details they cover inevitably become obsolete. The chapter I wrote about the Internet for the first edition of this book bears very little resemblance to this one. My focus this time around will be on general principles that will probably not change too much rather than the specifics, which probably will.

THE STATE OF THE WEB

The terms "World Wide Web" and "Internet" are used almost interchangeably today. But the Internet came first. The Web can be considered as simply a way of using the Internet. What we know as the Internet began in 1969 as the ARPAnet project of the Department of Defense. What emerged from this project was a worldwide network of computers—an "Internet." Until the mid-1990s and the emergence of the Web, the Internet was a user-unfriendly system with no graphics. The unbelievable growth in the popularity of the Internet is most likely due to the development of the Web as a graphical way of using this worldwide computer network.

The main problem with the Web at this stage in its development is its disorganization and preponderance of useless information. Picture a big library in which the books are not arranged by call number, just sort of grouped together loosely by subject. This can make it difficult to find the exact location of the material you need. Also, there are no librarians selecting books for quality; anything and everything is thrown in—elementary school compositions and high school book reports along with doctoral dissertations and works by Pulitzer Prize-winning authors. In addition, you are bombarded with advertising. This gets worse with each passing holiday season as "e-commerce" seems to emerge as the Web's reason for being.

Much of what you find, you find accidentally. If you are looking for something specific, you can often become quite frustrated. Imagine channel surfing on your TV hoping that you will find a program about your topic. I don't mean to sound completely negative. I have found some wonderful information on the Web and consider it, at its best, to be an amazing research tool.

But using the Web also presents technical problems. You may click on a link only to find that a resource is not found or no longer available. A Website may be available one day and gone the next. Graphics may take a long time to load. Response time may also be slow because too many users are trying to access the same site. Technical difficulties, however, will certainly become less bothersome as the Web is developed and matures from the infant stage it is now in.

THE STRUCTURE OF THE WEB

Think of the Web once again like a library full of books. Each Website is like one book. Just as a book has a table of contents, a Website has a *homepage*—an introductory page from which to begin your exploring. Most Websites consist of more than one page. Your school's homepage probably allows you to connect to all the different departmental pages, as well as pages about events, services, and the library. A page is a misleading term because the Web does not confine the designer of a Website to a certain amount of space. Pages can be of all different lengths. A page on the Web is defined as the space that you can scroll through at a particular address.

In addition to providing information, most Web pages also contain *links* to other Web pages. You can access other pages by clicking on these hypertext links. Links can be either highlighted text or a graphical image, or a graphic that incorporates text. To extend our book metaphor, let's say you're looking in a book for information on your topic. You could read the book from cover to cover in a linear fashion, or you could check the index in the back of the book to determine which pages contain the specific information you need. While looking in the index, you might see related topics listed with their appropriate page numbers. Referring to these different pages and flipping back and forth in a book using the index is the hypertextual way to read. But the Web takes it a step further. Imagine looking in the bibliography at the end of a book and instantly being able to get your hands on the books and articles cited. This is the sort of thing that Web page links allow you to do, and why this interwoven network of computers was probably named the World Wide Web in the first place.

You use browsing software to view Websites. *Netscape* is one of the most popular Web browsers. But there are other browsers such as Microsoft's *Internet Explorer*. Depending on which browser you use, the same Web page might look different if viewed from two computers using different software. Just as two different editions of *Moby Dick* might look different but contain exactly the same text, the content of the Website remains the same.

THE CONTENT OF THE WEB

The Web resources that are the focus of this chapter differ from all the other Web-based sources in this book because they are freely accessible to anyone who has access to the Web. In a figurative sense, no toll is required. As with just about anything that appears to be free, however, there are often hidden costs in the form of advertising and propaganda.

What can you find on the Web? That's like asking what you can see on a cross-country road trip. Because of the sheer bulk of information available, only some broad generalizations can be offered here based on the categories of information providers.

- Companies provide a lot of information about their products and services on the Web; mostly this is just advertising, but sometimes such information can be helpful. If you're researching a company, you will certainly want to take a look at its Website. With the rise of "e-commerce," many commercial sites are not only sources of information but interactive sites where customers can purchase products and perform transactions.

- Non-profit organizations also have a strong presence on the Web. These organizations are formed to promote a cause so their sites are designed to help in their mission. No matter how altruistic this mission is, watch out for propaganda and bias when viewing these sites. They're certainly not out to make a buck the way the commercial sites blatantly are, but they often have an agenda.

- Educational Institutions—Just about every college and university has a Website now. Many secondary schools and even elementary schools are going online with their own sites as well. Access to your library's Web-based resources is usually provided through your school's site. In addition to lots of information about events, student services, courses, and individual departments, colleges often let students and faculty post their own personal pages. While these can be excellent sources for research, be careful to evaluate the material as detailed in the next chapter. You might have at your disposal the wisdom of a world-renowned expert in Shakespearean studies who has made his research available to the world with no thought of financial gain. Or, at the other end of the spectrum, you might be able to view a fraternity site that explains how to make your own beer.

- Governmental Departments and Agencies—Since the Internet originated back in the late 1960s as a project of the Department of Defense, the United States government has always had a strong presence in cyberspace. As mentioned in Chapter 4, governmental sites can be wonderful, objective sources of information and provide lots of statistics, reports, etc. Take advantage of your tax dollars (or your parents' tax dollars) hard at work!

- Personal Websites—Personal sites can often be identified by a tilde (~) in the address. This category of site can be the biggest offender in the amount of junk on the Web. Although the other categories of sites usually have some form of editorial control because there is a higher organization to which the Web page author has to answer, personal pages can contain anything: from pornography to cookie recipes. Be extremely cautious when using personal sites, and make sure that the original source of any secondary information is clearly cited.

FINDING INFORMATION ON THE WEB

Website Addresses

Addresses, also sometimes called URLs or *uniform resource locators*, are entered in the location box of your browser in order to access a particular Web page. Homepages generally begin with *www* (although I am starting to see more and more which don't) and end with a three-letter code that gives an indication of the source of the information:

- **.com**—commercial sites
- **.org**—non-profit organizations
- **.edu**—educational institutions
- **.gov**—government agencies
- **.net**—internet service providers
- **.mil**—military sites

More specific addresses for other pages in a Website are lengthier and often more complicated. The address for a Web page is equivalent to the call number for a book. If you know it, you can easily find the source. The problem is that you have to get an address from another source—a friend, a magazine, a television commercial, a librarian, etc.

"Surfing"

Surfing is basically a process of clicking on Web page links. As an example of surfing, take a look at Figure 8.1, a page

Figure 8.1: A page from NASA's Website.

from NASA's Website that gives a brief history of the ill-fated Apollo 13 mission.

Notice in the second line under "Mission Objective" that the word "moon" is highlighted. When you click on this highlighted term, you can immediately access a Website with information about the moon, as displayed in Figure 8.2.

This Website has nothing to do with NASA; it's maintained by a software engineer named Bill Arnett who lives in Arizona and is interested in astronomy. From this site, if you were to click on the name Artemis, you'll be taken to another Website at an altogether different location that discusses Greek mythology. This is the nature of hypertext and what makes the Web so enticing. Although it gives you the freedom to jump around and follow various topics that may only have loose connections, it's really just like wandering around a library that isn't organized very well and haphazardly opening up books.

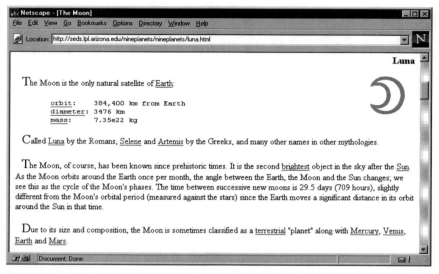

Figure 8.2: A page from "The Nine Planets: A Multimedia Tour of the Solar System" by Bill Arnett.

Search Engine Overview

Websites that are specifically designed to help you find other sites are called *search engines*. Using search engines to find Websites can loosely be compared to using an online catalog to find books. The purpose of this section is not to explain how to use each one. That would be quite futile considering how much they change, and also impossible considering the sheer number of them. There are close to 3,000 search engines listed in *www.searchengineguide.com*! But I would like you to understand the common features that search engines share. Table 8.1 gives you an overview of the major search engines currently available. A great site to go to for finding out the latest developments and news about search engines is *www.searchenginewatch.com*.

Despite the variety of search engines, they all provide a search box in which you can enter your terms, and, in return, get a list of links to sites which contain these terms.

Table 8.1: The Major Web Search Engines

- **About.com** (*www.about.com*)—a directory distinguished by its team of professional human "guides," each of whom is an expert in one of the 650+ subject areas covered.

- **AltaVista** (*www.altavista.com*)—one of the oldest and largest search engines in terms of pages covered; incorporates the Looksmart directory (see below) into its homepage.

- **Ask Jeeves** (*www.askjeeves.com*)—a search service run by real people which utilizes natural language searching.

- **Direct Hit** (*www.directhit.com*)—utilizes popularity ranking of sites retrieved; a directory is provided.

- **Dogpile** (*www.dogpile.com*)—a meta-search engine.

- **Excite** (*www.excite.com*)—medium-sized in terms of Web pages covered but one of the most popular; like AltaVista, it supplements its search service with direct access to the LookSmart directory.

- **GoTo** (*www.goto.com*)—companies can pay GoTo to have their links appear higher in the search results.

- **Google** (*www.google.com*)—a medium-sized search engine that ranks links by popularity; has the most uncluttered homepage of any of the major commercial search engines.

- **HotBot** (*www.hotbot.com*)—like AltaVista in its breadth of coverage; primary results are provided by Direct Hit, while the directory is provided by Open Directory.

- **Inference Find** (*www.infind.com*)—a meta-search engine that lists results by subject rather than by search engine.

- **Librarians' Index to the Internet** (*www.lii.org*)—here's a site to go to if you get sick of advertising and consumer-oriented search engines; provides a directory designed by highly selective librarians.

Continued

Table 8.1: *Continued*

- **LookSmart** (*www.looksmart.com*)—a directory compiled by humans that is also incorporated into a number of other search engines.

- **Lycos** (*www.lycos.com*)—a smaller search engine that supplements its results with the LookSmart directory.

- **Northern Light** (*www.northernlight.com*)—one of the largest search engines, it is distinguished by its feature of grouping the results into folders by topic. Also has a special collection of articles from periodicals and other sources that are available for a small fee.

- **Open Directory** (*www.opendirectory.com*)—a human-compiled directory covering over one million sites.

- **Savvy Search** (*www.savvysearch.com*)—a meta-search engine.

- **Snap.com** (*www.snap.com*)—a human-compiled directory covering over 600,000 sites.

- **WebCrawler** (*www.webcrawler.com*)—covers a small number of Websites; not good for obscure information but might be less overwhelming for broader topics.

- **WWW Virtual Library** (*www.vlib.org*)—another site to visit if you get tired of the consumer-oriented search engines; this is mainly a searchable directory maintained by volunteers that covers a wide range of topics.

- **Yahoo!** (*www.yahoo.com*)—the most popular search service, covering over one million sites. The original Web directory.

Unfortunately, most search engines are becoming so filled with banner ads, shopping guides, and other commercial material, that it's hard to know exactly what to do once you get to one of them. Take a look, for example, at the homepage of Snap.com displayed in Figure 8.3.

Figure 8.3: Snap.com's homepage.

The search box gets buried in all the clutter of the screen. As search engines such as Snap.com emerge that incorporate a variety of resources and services, including Web directories, free e-mail, news, chat rooms, and online shopping, a new term has come into usage—"portal sites." The emphasis of these portals seems to be on commercial purposes rather than academic research. You can get very distracted by all the opportunities to buy things, chat with people, and check out the latest news.

Search Engine Directories

Although I compared search engines to online book catalogs, there is a major difference. Records in an online catalog have a standard format and are assigned subject headings, which

Figure 8.4: Yahoo!'s homepage.

make it easy to access all of the items on a certain topic once you have determined what the appropriate headings are. Search engines search by keywords; as always, this means that your searching must always be imprecise.

Many search engines, however, incorporate directories that arrange sites hierarchically into various categories so that you can browse if your topic is fairly broad rather than enter keywords in the search box. This is as close as search engines come to assigning subject headings to sites. If you refer back to Figure 8.3, you will see that Snap.com has a Web Directory providing a number of consumer-oriented categories. I prefer the popular Yahoo! directory, which categorizes over one million Websites under a small number of main headings on its homepage, as seen in Figure 8.4. Ya-

Figure 8.5: Yahoo!'s "Arts & Humanities" directory.

hoo! is one of the oldest directories on the Web. Most of the other search engines have copied its idea of providing a list of categories and assigning sites to these categories.

Clicking on one of Yahoo!'s main headings will bring you to another page that lists the subheadings for this broad topic. For example, let's say you wanted to take a look at the Websites of various modern-art museums. Click on the first category in the directory, "Arts & Humanities." This brings up the screen displayed in Figure 8.5.

From this screen, select "Museums, Galleries, and Centers." The next screen to appear is shown in Figure 8.6, which lists narrower subheadings, including "Modern and Contemporary."

Notice that below the list of subheadings, links to individual museums have appeared. Click on any of these and you will go to the site of the museum listed. These links fit into many different categories. But because you specifically want to view the links for modern-art museums, you would have to select that option from the list of headings at the top portion of the screen.

What Are You Searching?

At this point it is important to understand that there is no search engine that covers the entire Web. Even meta-search engines, which are sites allowing you to search multiple engines simultaneously, don't cover every single page. Each engine covers a different range of sites just as each online catalog covers a different collection of resources. Although

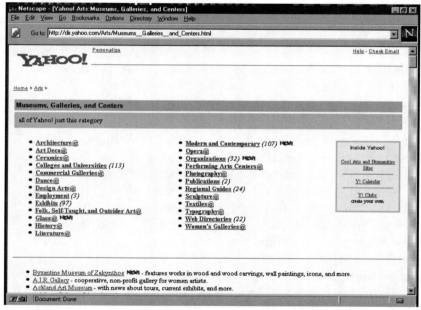

Reprinted with permission of Yahoo! Inc. © 1999 by Yahoo! Inc. YAHOO! and the YAHOO! logo are trademarks of Yahoo! Inc.

Figure 8.6: Yahoo!'s "Museums, Galleries, and Centers" directory.

I don't want to get technical, in order to evaluate which one to use, you should understand the two basic ways that search engines select the sources to be covered.

Sites are either evaluated by human beings for inclusion or the process is automated by computers. Yahoo!, for example, employs a team of people to find acceptable sites and then assign a category to each one. Yahoo! also accepts submissions from users, which are evaluated by their team for inclusion. There are a number of other search engines, including Snap.com, LookSmart, and About.com, that use human evaluation for site selection.

Then you have the big search engines like AltaVista and Lycos that include so many sites that the whole process of selection must be automated. The big search engines send out electronic "spiders" to go to sites and add them to the database. Then the spiders follow all the links on the initial sites and add all of those secondary sites, and so on. The big search engines that boast the number of pages they index rely on quantity while the smaller directories prefer quality. This difference is important when it comes to evaluating the results of your search.

The lesson to be learned is that if your topic is somewhat broad, you might want to use a search engine that covers fewer sites and employs some selection criteria (e.g., Yahoo! or WebCrawler). On the other hand, if your topic is a bit more obscure, you may want to use one of the larger search engines like AltaVista or Northern Light.

Searching Techniques

Much of what you learned about searching a database in Chapters 2 and 7 relates to searching the Web, so I won't give a lot of examples in this section. Most search engines have "help" pages that provide you with tips and examples. Like just about all the databases we've seen in this book, there are both basic and advanced ways of using Web search engines. But most search engine users never get beyond en-

Figure 8.7: Lycos' advanced search page.

tering a string of keywords in the search box and than browsing through the often lengthy list of links retrieved, most of them irrelevant to their needs.

First of all, you can use Boolean connecting terms in Web search engines. The ways in which you do this differ from engine to engine. But generally, if you enter a string of keywords, the term OR is implied between them. So the more keywords you enter, the more results you will get, although many of them will be far off target in regard to your topic. Because the term OR is implied, an almost universal rule is that, in order to find an exact phrase, you must enter it within quotation marks. If you were to enter **Ricky Martin** in a search engine without quotation marks, you would retrieve, among many other things, sites that mention Ricky Ricardo and others about Steve Martin. Web search engines also use truncation and often no symbol is required so that any variant endings of the words you enter will be retrieved automatically. Some engines, however, such as Yahoo!, require the asterisk. Others require you to go to an advanced search page.

As we have seen before, one way to make your search more precise is to use AND. In many search engines, you specify AND by putting a plus sign before a term. Conversely, if you want to eliminate a term from your search, you enter a minus sign to signify NOT. For example, if you enter the following search: **+titanic +sinking –movie** in just about any of the search engines, you will increase your chances of finding sites concerned with the demise of the real ship rather than the silver screen version.

In some search engines there is an advanced search page that employs pull-down menus to facilitate the searching process. As you can see in Figure 8.7, Lycos provides a pull-down menu that lets you choose from the following options: "all words" for AND, "any words" for OR, or "exact phrase."

In Snap.com, which, despite its cluttered homepage, has a very nice advanced search page as shown in Figure 8.8, the options are similar to those in Lycos. In addition, you can limit your search to the page title or perform a truncated search by selecting "All forms of the word." You can also limit your search by date and language.

Many other advanced search pages provide limitations such as date and language. Additionally, some sites, such as Northern Light, let you specify if you want to limit your search to commercial sites, educational sites, organizational sites, etc. Northern Light's "Power Search" page is displayed in Figure 8.9.

Natural language searching is also becoming popular in Web search engines such as Ask Jeeves and Northern Light. As mentioned in the previous chapter, when natural language searching you enter a question to which you need an answer; the search engine eliminates any extraneous terms and then searches for the others, ranking the results by relevance. If

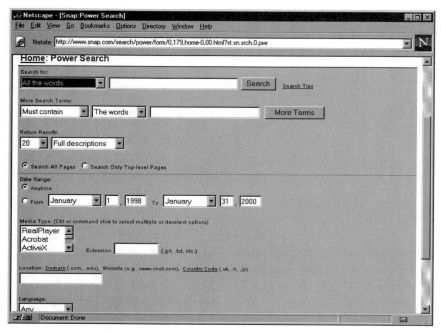

Figure 8.8: Snap.com's "Power Search" page.

you're lucky, this type of search can be effective, but I think it can often be inefficient.

Order of Websites Found

When you do a keyword search in an online catalog, your list of books is usually displayed in alphabetical order. When you receive a list of Website links in response to your search engine query, what order are they displayed in? Some search engines employ relevancy ranking that orders sites retrieved by the frequency of search terms. In other words, sites that contain all of your words in the greatest quantity will appear at the top of the list. Other search engines rank sites by popularity. Direct Hit and Google rank sites by popularity so that, in response to your search for a topic, the sites

Figure 8.9: Northern Light's "Power Search" page.

that have been visited the most by other users on this topic will appear first. The reasoning is that the most useful sites will emerge since users have, in a way, voted for them. Then there is a deceptive type of ranking which is linked to fees paid by Websites to search engines. For example, GoTo allows companies to pay a fee so that their sites will appear higher in the list than others. I don't consider this practice appropriate for any search engine that is to be used for academic research.

Search Engine Recommendations

I can't tell you definitively which search engine is best. There are so many, I honestly have not had time to evaluate each one as thoroughly as I'd like to. You will develop your own personal favorites just as I have, based on your success rate and your comfort level. It's best to choose a couple that you like—perhaps one for broad searches and one for narrower topics—and focus on learning how to use them well. Table 8.1 provides you with a list of the major search engines along with their addresses and some brief notes on each.

As for my personal preferences, I like Yahoo! for subjects of a general nature or when I'm in the mood to browse a bit. For more specific searches, I have had good luck with Northern Light, which organizes the sites found into more specific subject folders rather than as one long list. I tend to stay away from the highly consumer-oriented search engines—the ones with so much advertising that you can hardly find the search box. I hardly ever use meta-search engines except out of curiosity. I think they are best reserved for the narrowest topics; otherwise, you are likely to be overwhelmed by information.

Many of the Websites you find may contain pages that say "Under Construction." In a way, the entire Web is under construction, and by its nature will always be a "work in progress," just as the highway system must continually be maintained with new roads being built and old ones paved over. The tools used to search the Web are also under construction. So, be prepared for a bumpy ride and, as I advised you in the beginning of this chapter, proceed with caution. But enjoy the ride because you will certainly see some unexpected things.

Nine

The Trip Home

After a long road trip I like to think back upon where I've been and what I've seen. I might make some evaluations about what I liked and didn't like and if I'd want to travel the same route again in the future. I often feel compelled to write about my travels in order to preserve a record of the trip.

We've traveled a long road together since the beginning of this book. Along the way I've given you many directions, pointed out many sights, and tried to impart to you a sense of familiarity with the world of research. With this background, I hope you feel prepared to take the wheel confidently and travel through the library—both real and virtual.

Whenever I'm lost on the road, however, I don't wander around too long before I stop for directions. I figure I can save a lot of time and frustration if I simply ask someone for help. In the same way, you should not hesitate to ask for help in your library. Even after reading this book you may find that there are times when you feel a bit lost. That's understandable, and that's why every library has a reference desk where you can go to find your way amid all the resources available.

EVALUATING WHAT YOU'VE FOUND

Doing research is not just about finding information, it's also about evaluating what you've found and determining what will be useful. This is especially critical when it comes to Web resources. With the constantly increasing amount of information available and the powerful electronic tools we now have for accessing it, you may well discover, to your surprise and dismay, that you've overwhelmed yourself with too many resources.

Although I've placed this section on evaluation here at the end of this book, evaluating your sources should actually be an ongoing process rather than something you do after you've found everything on your topic. Evaluation focuses on four main points: authority, content, accuracy, and currency. This is true for books, articles, Websites—any information.

Authority: Who Wrote It?

An author with credentials or some sort of track record adds credibility to a resource. While you can't always find out much about the author, books usually contain brief biographies. With periodicals, remember that you don't want to rely exclusively on popular magazines. Articles from scholarly journals carry more weight and are generally written by experts in their field. Plus, these articles have often been selected by the authors' peers as worthy of publication.

When it comes to evaluating the authority of Websites, however, the problem is that anyone can put up a Website. Many sites have absolutely no editorial control. It is important to know who is behind the information that you see on a Web page. This can sometimes be more difficult than with print resources. The author is not always identified. The Webmaster, Webmistress, or Webspinner who may be named at the bottom of the page is not necessarily the same person as the author of the content; rather, this person designs and/or maintains the site.

You can tell a lot about a Website simply from its address. As explained in the last chapter, addresses ending in .com are commercial sites. Such sites are usually trying to sell something; they are just advertising in disguise. Keep this in mind when evaluating the informational content of the site. Addresses ending in .org are put up by non-profit organizations. Therefore, it is likely that the purpose of the site is to promote the cause of the organization. This bias will add a certain slant to the information. Sites affiliated with educational institutions end in .edu. You might think that the information included in such sites would be free of propaganda, but think again. Also, look out for students' personal pages. You can identify a personal page because it usually contains a tilde (~). The problem with such pages is that there is absolutely no editorial control. They may contain bad poetry, family photos, or Junior's A+ science paper.

Content: Does It Adequately Address My Topic?

Perhaps the most fundamental question you should ask is whether each source adequately provides you with the information you need. Does it answer the main questions that you have about your topic? The records you find using indexes and online book catalogs do not always have enough information to evaluate the material cited. Even when you are given an abstract in an article citation or a table of contents in an online book record, you may not get a clear idea of what the source will really provide. The only way to do this is to get your hands on the actual book or article and skim through it, noticing how extensively your topic is addressed. You might also want to look up your topic in the book's index to get a sense of how many pages are devoted to it. Even though the source may have sounded great initially, you may realize that it won't really help you. Don't select a source for the sake of having one more item to add to your bibliography or just because it is easier to get. The quality of your information is more important than the quantity.

As I've touched upon previously, the best material may not always be the easiest information to get your hands on. For example, you might have to go to microfilm to get an old newspaper article or use a print index in order to find articles from the pre-computer days. Although I certainly appreciate the information superhighway that has been created by computers, I also see the value of the informational "back roads." Even though the highway can be very useful when your primary goal is to get somewhere fast, it is often more interesting to explore the back roads when you have the time.

Accuracy: Is the Information Correct?

Accuracy is related to content and is most applicable to evaluating Websites. A book or article should have gone through an editorial process that will have involved fact-checking, while Websites, as I'm sure is clear by now, are often unedited and as a result contain a lot of erroneous information. But print resources are not perfect either. If you have found a number of articles and books and gained a working knowledge of your subject, you may have learned enough to notice inaccuracies in some of your print resources too. If you detect numerous inaccuracies in a resource, you may want to reconsider using it.

Even if you notice minor errors like misspellings, you should be cautious because this reflects poorly on the source as a whole. Here's an interesting example which points out the weakness of the Web as compared to edited print sources. Using the Northern Light search engine one evening late in 1999, I looked up the term "millennium" and found over one million references. Then I misspelled the term "millenium" and still found almost 350,000! That's an error rate of over thirty percent. Next, I searched for "millennium" in EBSCOhost's *Academic Search* and found over five thousand articles; the erroneous "millenium" retrieved fewer than 200. The error rate for published periodicals covered by this index was a relatively respectable 3.5 percent.

Currency: When Was It Written?

Sometimes it's important to have the most recent information available, especially for scientific and business-related topics. In such cases, as you search for material on your subject, you should keep in mind the date each item was written. This will help you to narrow your search and focus on the most valuable information. At other times, it is not necessary to have the most up-to-date material, particularly with historical, social science, and humanities topics. In fact, when researching such areas, the latest information may not be the best.

Most students, however, prefer more recent information, particularly periodical articles, because it is usually easier to obtain. As I pointed out, most of the older stuff is on microfilm and to find citations for this material you may have to use a print index rather than an electronic one. With the emerging availability of recent full-text articles online, more people are opting for current information. While I have nothing against the convenience of full-text electronic sources, I have observed that too many students rely exclusively on the limited sources available in this format. Let me once again remind you that, just like cruising historic Route 66 is much more interesting than speeding along on Interstate 40, sometimes the most interesting sites are off the beaten track. So don't always look for the fastest way to get the most recent information. You may miss out on some really good sources.

It's easy enough to determine the date that a book was

written. The copyright date will be on one of the first few left-hand pages. It will also be listed in the online catalog record. The dates for articles are included in the citations you found through indexes. Finding out how old a Website is can be problematic (like so many things about the Web) because Websites are constantly updated. If the Website designer has followed the rules of good design and maintenance, the date when the site was last updated should appear prominently on the homepage as well as on each page that has been revised within the site. Even if a date does appear on a Website, however, you often have no way of knowing if it is the date of initial creation or the date of most recent revision.

THE RECORD OF YOUR TRIP: CITING YOUR SOURCES

Of course, the end product of all your research and the record of your trip is reflected in the paper or project that you complete for your class. This book is not intended to teach you how to actually write the paper, but an important component of your paper is the documentation that gives credit to the sources you used to write it. Students frequently ask librarians how to cite resources, so I'd like to briefly discuss this.

There is no single method of citing sources. Your professor may request that you follow a certain format. The rules laid out in *The Chicago Manual of Style*'s chapter on documentation are often specified, or your professor might suggest Kate Turabian's *A Manual for Writers of Term Papers, Theses, and Dissertations*, which follows the same rules as *Chicago*. Two other common formats are the MLA (Modern Language Association) style and the APA (American Psychological Association) style. To learn how to use these styles, you should be able to find the following handbooks in your library: *The MLA Handbook for Writers of Research Papers* and *The Publication Manual of the American Psychological Association.* Either of these books will show you in great detail how to cite just about anything you could possibly want to cite. More recent editions include rules on citing electronic resources. No matter which style you choose, the important thing is to maintain consistency. In other words, if you use MLA for one citation, you must use MLA for all.

The list of sources that you should include at the end of your paper is generically referred to as a bibliography. When using MLA style, however, you title this page "Works Cited," while according to APA it is called "References." But if you're using the *Chicago* style, just call it the "Bibliography." In addition to a bibliography, you need to incorporate notes into your paper. Immediately after you use a direct quote or paraphrase the thought of someone else, you must give credit to the source—including the exact page reference.

With *Chicago* style, you either use footnotes or endnotes. A superscript number is inserted at the end of the passage you want to cite. Then you either include a citation as a footnote at the bottom of the page or collect all your citations together as endnotes at the end of the paper. Unlike bibliography citations, these are more specific, usually citing the exact page numbers. When using APA or MLA style you don't use footnotes or endnotes. Instead you use parenthetical citations; for example, if you quote what Dr. Smith wrote on page 2 of his book, you just insert (Smith, 2) after the quote.

The purpose of citing sources is to give credit to the authors of the sources you used, to give credibility to the facts you state in your paper, and to enable anyone who reads your paper to locate these sources. It is very important to include accurate information and double-check all your citations.

In the next few pages, I'll provide you with some general guidelines on how to cite the main categories of material: books, periodical articles, and Websites. I'll use examples that follow *Chicago* style, which seems most common in undergraduate research papers. Just consult the APA or MLA style guides if your professor prefers one or the other. And if you do use *Chicago* style, you'll need to consult *The Chicago Manual of Style* if your sources vary from the examples discussed here.

Citing Books

The basic components of a book citation are the author, the title, the publisher, and the place and date of publication. For example, here is a typical citation for a book using *The Chicago Manual of Style*:

> Nelson, Rob. *Revolution X: A Survival Guide for Our Generation*. New York: Penguin Books, 1994.

Suppose that within your paper, you also specifically quoted something written on page 95 of Nelson's book. Following *Chicago* style, you have to provide a footnote or endnote; this has a slightly different format than the bibliographic citation above:

> 1. Rob Nelson, *Revolution X: A Survival Guide for Our Generation* (New York: Penguin Books, 1994), 95.

Notice that the author's name is not inverted and that the citation is indented. There are also subtle differences in punctuation—commas instead of periods and parentheses around the publisher and date. If you cite the same source more than once in your paper, *Chicago* style gets a little easier. Let's say that the footnote immediately following the one above cites something Nelson said on page 143. There is no need to repeat the entire citation, you would just use:

"ibid., 143." Ibid. stands for "ibidem," which in Latin means "in the same place." If there were an intervening footnote, however, you would have to use a shortened citation omitting the subtitle and all but the most essential information: "Nelson, *Revolution X*, 143."

There are many variations for citing books: your book may have two, three, or more authors, or no author but instead an editor, as in the case of many reference works. It could be a multivolume work or a specific edition. In each of these cases, the citation is a little different, so refer to *The Chicago Manual of Style* for guidance.

Citing Periodical Articles

By now you should be familiar with the basic components of a periodical article citation since they are included in all indexes: the author, the title of the article, the title of the periodical in which the article is published, the date of the issue, page numbers, and, in the case of a journal, the volume and issue numbers.

The format for your bibliography, however, is a bit different from what you've seen in indexes. Here's a sample bibliography citation for an article in a popular magazine using *The Chicago Manual of Style*:

Fischoff, Stuart. "Confessions of a TV Talk Show Shrink." *Psychology Today*, Sept./Oct. 1995, 38–45.

If you are citing a journal article, you must also include the volume and issue numbers, so the format would follow the example below:

Wexler, Mark N., and Ron Smith. "The Psycho-Social Significance of Trivia." *Journal of Popular Culture* 28, no. 2 (1994): 1–11.

The citation above indicates that the article is in issue 2 of volume 28, pages 1 through 11. I don't want this chapter to get too lengthy, so if you want to see examples of foot-notes and endnotes for periodicals, there are plenty in *The Chicago Manual of Style*.

What if you got the text of an article online, perhaps through InfoTrac or EBSCOhost? The citation format has to reflect this. Let's say you found the *Psychology Today* article online on EBSCOhost's *MasterFILE Premier*. Here's how you would cite it using *Chicago* style:

Fischoff, Stuart. "Confessions of a TV Talk Show Shrink." *Psychology Today*, Sept./Oct. 1995, 38+. In *MasterFILE Premier* [online database]; available: www.epnet.com/ehost/login.html (Boston, MA: EBSCO Publishing, accessed 15 Dec 1999).

The rules regarding electronic citation are not set in stone like those for more traditional resources. Always refer to the most recent edition of the style guides for more specific instructions. In general, you must indicate what online service you used, what company produces it, the Web address of the service's homepage, and the date you accessed it. Page numbers are irrelevant when it comes to Web versions of articles. The online citation usually gives the number of the first page and sometimes the length of the article as it appeared in print. In the example above, "38+" is accurate because EBSCOhost indicates that the article is eight pages long, but it is not clear if this is eight continuous pages or if the article skips around.

Citing Websites

The rules for citing Web pages or sites are similar to those for citing electronic versions of print articles. If you recall that one of the fundamental purposes of citing resources is so others can find them, then the information you should include makes sense. Although the rules are still under development, some general guidelines can be given here. I found a site that interprets *Chicago* style for online citations. Using the rules there, I composed the following bibliographic citation for this site.

> Harnack, Andrew, and Eugene Kleppinger. "Using Chicago Style to Cite and Document Sources." *Online!: A Reference Guide to Using Internet Sources*. 1998. <www.bedfordstmartins.com/online/ cite7.html#1> (20 December 1999).

As you can see I included the following:

- Author's name—basically, whoever is responsible for the content; this could be an individual or an organization. If no author is indicated, you'll just have to leave this out.
- Title of the Web page and/or Website—to understand the difference, here is an analogy: a Web page is like a chapter in a book, while a Website is like the entire book. Remember a Web page's length is not confined to a certain size as a printed book is.
- Date the page was created (or date of most recent update).
- Address—the complete URL (be very careful to double-check; sometimes these can be long).
- Date visited—when you accessed it.

LOOKING BACK ON THE ROAD

Just to make sure that you're headed the right way as you finish this book, let's review the basic directions I've given for doing effective research:

- First, you need to know where you're going and what you're looking for. Define your topic. If possible, pick a topic that interests you, just as you would choose a vacation destination for its appeal. Plan your route by determining what types of sources you need, how you will find them, and roughly how much time it will take you. Don't procrastinate!

- Start by searching the online catalog for books. If you have problems with subject searching try keyword searching using the basic principles of Boolean logic.
- Go to the stacks and locate the books whose records you found on the computer. If you need more books, do some "educated browsing" or consider using the collections of other libraries.
- Consult some basic reference sources if you need to check a fact or get some background information.
- Locate periodical articles on your topic using online and CD-ROM indexes; use print indexes for older articles.
- Determine what indexes are available at your library and in what format, then select the most appropriate ones for your topic.
- If you find too many articles, narrow your search; if you find too few, broaden your search utilizing the principles outlined in Chapter 7.
- Search the Web last. If you have acquired a knowledge of your topic from books and articles, you will be better able to evaluate the accuracy of Web resources. Remember that there's a lot of junk out there. The most effective way to find what you need on the Web is to use search engines, particularly the advanced search screens.

EPILOGUE: RIDING OFF INTO THE SUNSET

On a road trip, you may travel hundreds, even thousands, of miles for days, maybe weeks. You might think you've covered a lot of territory. But if you take a look at a globe, you'll realize how little of the world you've actually seen. Even if you spend your lifetime traveling you'll never see it all.

It's the same with information. Consider, for example, that approximately fifty thousand books are published each year in the United States alone. Over ten thousand magazines and journals are currently in print. There are currently an estimated eight-hundred million Web pages and this number is growing exponentially each year. Walking into an average-sized library and looking at all the books on the shelves can be intimidating but at the same time invigorating. Just as you will never be able to explore every nook and cranny on Earth, you will never be able to absorb all the information available—the accumulated knowledge of the human race.

The important thing is to be able to pinpoint the specific information that addresses your needs. Having read this book, I hope you will now be able to do this more efficiently, saving yourself lots of time and frustration so that you can more fully enjoy your time at college. If you get your research done more efficiently, as you should using the techniques I have described in this book, maybe you can reward yourself for a job well done by taking a real road trip. And when you leave college, you'll have the skills that are essential in this "information age" we live in.

Bon voyage!

Index

About the Author

Arlene Quaratiello is a reference librarian at Merrimack College in North Andover, Massachusetts. She has also worked at Emerson College in Boston as the Coordinator of Library Instruction. She received her MLS from Simmons College and earned a degree in English from the College of the Holy Cross. Arlene has written articles for a number of publications including *RQ*, *Computers in Libraries*, and *C&RL News*. She is also a professional book indexer. Originally from New Jersey, she now lives in Atkinson, New Hampshire, with her husband Mark and daughter Grace.